A Students' Guide to Programming in

pascal

Laurence V. Atkinson

Department of Computer Science,
The University of Sheffield,
Sheffield, S10 2TN

JOHN WILEY & SONS
Chichester · New York · Brisbane · Toronto · Singapore

Reprinted with corrections April 1983
Reprinted January 1984
Reprinted February 1985
Reprinted January 1986

British Library Cataloguing in Publication Data:

Atkinson, Laurence V.
  A students' guide to programming in Pascal.
  1. PASCAL (Computer program language)
  I. Title
  001.64'24   QA76.73.P2

  ISBN 0 471 10402 7

Printed in Great Britain

£6·50

A Students' Guide to Programming in Pascal

Contents

Foreword

This book presents an introduction to the computer programming language Pascal and is the basis of a sixteen-part video series PROGRAMMING IN PASCAL, produced by the University of Sheffield Television Service and available both from John Wiley & Sons and from Guild Sound and Vision. Each video session lasts approximately half an hour and corresponds to one chapter in this book. The order of presentation of examples in the video series usually follows that of the book but some are omitted and, because of the size constraints of a television screen, some have been slightly changed.

This book provides a more gentle introduction to Pascal than the Author's earlier book (PASCAL PROGRAMMING published by John Wiley & Sons 1980), gives less detailed discussion of topics and omits some advanced features of the language.

No previous computer experience or programming knowledge is assumed and so the book is suitable for complete beginners. No particular mathematical ability is required beyond a basic familiarity with numbers but, for the benefit of the mathematically inclined, a number of mathematical examples have been included. For the most part, these can be ignored by the non-mathematical reader.

Each chapter concludes with a number of exercises – and the only way to learn programming is by doing it, so have a go at them! If you do not have time to attempt all the exercises, try those marked with an asterisk; they form a representative sample.

The programming language Pascal is defined by a published standard

> BSI : Specification for
> Computer programming language Pascal
> (BS 6192 : 1982)

and all programs in this book conform to this standard. Some Pascal implementations, particularly those on microprocessors, do not. This is unfortunate because deviation from the standard implies that a program written on one computer may not run on another. If you are faced with a deviating implementation, you are advised to use only those features that conform to the standard.

Introduction

What is a computer? Well, if you have any preconceived notion that a computer is a fantastic brain with incredible intelligence and powers of reasoning - forget it! A computer is moronic, devoid of all reasoning power. It does exactly what we tell it to - no more and no less. If we tell it to do something stupid, it does it. If we tell it to do something impossible it will still have a go.

So why do we use these stupid machines? Well if we tell them to do sensible things, they do sensible things. They do them very very quickly and without making mistakes - and they are particularly good at doing things over and over again.

So how do we get a computer to do what we want it to? Well, a computer differs from most machines in two respects. With most machines we make them do what we want by pressing knobs, flicking switches and so on and the machine responds immediately. To tell a computer what we want it to do, we sit at a <u>keyboard</u> and type <u>instructions</u>; but the computer does not obey each instruction as we give it. Instead, it stores a whole sequence of instructions without obeying any of them.

When we have given the computer all the instructions we want to, we tell it to obey them and only then does it work its way through them. The sequence of instructions is called a <u>program</u>. So a computer differs from other machines in that it operates under the control of a stored program. The process of constructing (or writing) a program is called <u>programming</u> and that is what this book is all about.

A program can be prepared for a computer in one of two ways. The traditional approach is called <u>off-line</u>. The keyboard used to type the instructions is not connected to a computer but produces a machine-readable form (usually by punching holes in rectangular cards). A more popular approach is to prepare and run programs <u>on-line</u>. The user sits at a <u>terminal</u> connected directly to the computer. The terminal is like an electric typewriter but may have a display screen in place of paper, in which case it is called a <u>visual display unit</u> (or, simply, a VDU). I shall assume that you have access to a computer via a terminal and I shall adopt terminology applicable to a VDU. On a VDU, information is written in lines across the screen from the top to the bottom and the current printing position is indicated by some special character (possibly flashing) called the <u>cursor</u>.

So what form do our instructions take and what language do we use? You might think it would be nice if we could give our instructions in English or French or some other natural language but this turns out not to be a very good idea because natural languages are prone to ambiguities. Computers do exactly what we tell them to and so we must be very precise when we tell them. Special languages have been developed and a language used for writing programs is called a <u>programming</u> language. They are usually a sort of stylised English with a few special symbols thrown in. They are designed so that we can work at the level at which <u>we</u> want to think about things rather then at the level at which the machine must operate - so they are called <u>high</u> <u>level</u> languages.

Unfortunately, a program written in a high level language does not make much sense to a computer. Before it can be obeyed, it must be changed into a much simpler form; it must be translated into what is called <u>machine code</u> (and each computer has its own machine code). The translation process is called <u>compilation</u> and it is performed by the computer itself, using a program (a machine code program) called a <u>compiler</u>.

The original program, written in the high level language, is called the <u>source</u> program. The compiler takes this and produces an equivalent machine code program. This compiled program can then be obeyed (we usually say 'run' or 'executed'). So, on a computer, you can use any programming language for which the computer has a compiler.

There are many programming languages in existence but only a few have gained wide acceptance. Some are special purpose, each intended for one particular application area; some are general purpose. The language we are going to use is general purpose. It is called Pascal, named after the seventeenth century French mathematician, and it is available on almost every computer - from great big machines which might occupy the whole floor of a building, right down to tiny microprocessors.

Pascal is probably the best, widely available, general purpose programming language in the world at the present time, especially as a vehicle for learning the principles of good programming. That is why we are going to use it! It has three main advantages over most other languages and I will mention them briefly now.

First, <u>transparency</u> - a program is said to be transparent if it is easy to read and easy to understand. Given a well-written Pascal program we can easily see what its intended effect is.

Second, <u>efficiency</u> - this concerns the size of programs and the speed at which they run on the computer. To be efficient, a program should be small and fast. That is, the compiled version should be small and fast - it does not matter how long the Pascal source program is.

The third advantage, and the one which really distinguishes Pascal from its predecessors, is <u>security</u>. We all make mistakes and, as you will soon discover, this is rarely more apparent than when we are writing programs for a computer. But the nice thing about Pascal is that, if we write our programs well, the computer, and in particular the compiler, is more able to spot mistakes than if we had written the program in almost any other language - and, of course, because Pascal programs are transparent, we tend to make fewer mistakes anyway. So, in this context, security does not mean locking something away where no-one can get at it; it means that not much is likely to go wrong without being noticed.

In this book I hope to show you how to write Pascal programs which are transparent, efficient and secure.

CHAPTER 1
Getting Started

1.1 The form of a program

Pascal instructions are called statements. At its simplest, a Pascal program has the form

```
PROGRAM n (output);

BEGIN

    { statements }

END.

where n is a program name,
   invented by the programmer
```

A name in Pascal is called an identifier. An identifier may contain only letters and digits and must start with a letter. Some compilers regard only the first eight characters of an identifier to be significant and ignore the rest. Two identifiers you intend to be different should therefore differ in their first eight characters. Whenever you invent an identifier, always choose something meaningful.

PROGRAM, BEGIN and END are reserved words. This means that they can be used only in the context for which they are intended; they cannot serve as identifiers. Pascal does not distinguish upper and lower case letters and we can turn this to our advantage. To distinguish reserved words from identifiers we shall use upper case (capitals) for reserved words and (mainly) lower case for identifiers. Your terminal may not have small letters - in which case you will have to type all letters as capitals.

The first line of the program is called the program heading. The rest of the program is the program body. The identifier "output" within the program heading signifies that the program will produce output at the terminal. I have typed this with lower case letters because, as we shall see later, it is the name of something and not a reserved word.

At least one space or end-of-line must appear between adjacent identifiers, reserved words and numbers but none can occur within any symbol comprising more than one character. Additional spaces and ends of lines occurring between symbols are ignored.

In Pascal, successive statements are separated by semicolons. Notice that the program finishes with a full stop.

1.2 Output

If we are to see the effect of a program it must produce some output.

1.2.1 writeln

A line of output can be produced by a writeln-statement of the following
form

        writeln ('..........')

where the dots represent the sequence of characters we want to print.
The apostrophes are called string quotes and a sequence of characters
enclosed between string quotes is called a string. Here is an example of
a writeln-statement.

        writeln ('Merry Christmas')

     When a writeln-statement is obeyed at run-time, it prints the
string at the terminal so the following program

        PROGRAM Yuletide (output);
        BEGIN
            writeln ('Merry Christmas')
        END.

will print the message

        Merry Christmas

     To include a string quote within a string it must be typed twice.
The statement

        writeln ('this''ll work won''t it')

produces

        this'll work won't it

     One writeln-statement can be supplied with several strings if
successive strings are separated by commas so, for example, this is a
legal writeln-statement:

        writeln ('Merry', 'Christmas')

When the computer obeys a writeln-statement like this one, it only
prints the characters in the strings. It does not matter how many spaces
there are between the strings so the statement above will run the two
strings together like this:

        MerryChristmas

If we want a space in the output, we must have a space in one of the
strings; perhaps like this:

```
            writeln ('Merry ', 'Christmas')
```

One writeln-statement produces all its output on one line. To produce output on more than one line, we must use more than one writeln-statement and, as mentioned earlier, successive statements must be separated by a semicolon. The program

```
        PROGRAM Yuletide (output);
        BEGIN
            writeln ('Merry Christmas');
            writeln ('Happy New Year')
        END.
```

will produce two lines of output

```
        Merry Christmas
        Happy New Year
```

and this one

```
        PROGRAM NameAndAddress (output);
        BEGIN
            writeln ('Dr L V Atkinson');
            writeln ('Department of Computer Science');
            writeln ('  The University');
            writeln ('     Sheffield');
            writeln ('        S10 2TN')
        END.
```

will print five lines.

```
        Dr L V Atkinson
        Department of Computer Science
          The University
            Sheffield
               S10 2TN
```

The identifier "writeln" is the name of something known as a procedure and the strings we supply are known as parameters. When a writeln-statement is activated we are said to be calling the procedure. It is possible to call the procedure "writeln" with no parameters and then its effect at run-time is to print nothing; it simply moves the cursor down to the start of the next line. In the following program

```
        PROGRAM NameAndAddress (output);
        BEGIN
            writeln ('Dr L V Atkinson');
            writeln;
            writeln ('Department of Computer Science');
            writeln ('  The University');
            writeln ('     Sheffield');
            writeln ('        S10 2TN')
        END.
```

the effect of the parameterless writeln-statement is to produce a blank line between the name and the first line of the address.

Dr L V Atkinson

Department of Computer Science
The University
Sheffield
S10 2TN

1.2.2 write

A write-statement has the same form as a writeln-statement except that
"write" replaces "writeln" and at least one parameter must be supplied.
The effect at run-time is the same except that the current output line
is not terminated - output from successive write-statements appears on
the same line. A writeln-statement with three parameters "a", "b" and
"c"

        writeln (a, b, c)

is equivalent to the two statements

        write (a, b, c);   writeln

and these, in turn, are equivalent to the four statements

        write (a);   write (b);   write (c);   writeln

The usefulness of "write" will become apparent later.

1.3 Program layout

Spaces and ends of lines have no significance except within strings and
between adjacent identifiers, reserved words and numbers; they are
ignored by the compiler. To the human reader, however, their inclusion
is very important; neat layout is a major contributory factor towards
program transparency.

    We shall adopt certain layout conventions and you are advised to
follow suit. If you are lucky, your compiler might control the layout of
your printed programs automatically. Our conventions will become
apparent as new programming constructs are introduced; some have already
been illustrated.

    (a)   Nothing precedes PROGRAM, BEGIN or END on a line.
    (b)   PROGRAM, BEGIN and END are aligned but information between BEGIN
          and END (and, as we shall see later, between PROGRAM and BEGIN)
          is indented two or three spaces.
    (c)   A semicolon immediately follows the first of the two items it
          separates.
    (d)   Two statements on the same line are separated by a few spaces.
    (e)   A statement does not extend across a line boundary (but this
          constraint will be relaxed when statements get longer).

    Because a semicolon separates one statement from the next, no
semicolon should follow a statement which precedes END. However, a

semicolon at this point is allowed and some people find that its
inclusion simplifies the task of inserting further statements at a later
date. In this book, no such superfluous semicolons will appear.

1.4 Comments

It is often useful to annotate a program for the benefit of the human
reader. To this end, Pascal permits the inclusion of comments within a
program. It is customary to insert a comment at the head of a program to
describe the function of the program and perhaps give such information
as the names of the authors and the date the program was last amended.

Any sequence of characters enclosed between braces, the curly
brackets { and }, is interpreted as a comment and has no effect upon the
action of the program. If your computer character set does not include
braces, comments must be enclosed between the compound symbols (* and
*). A comment may appear at any point in your program at which a space
would be legal. Here is an example of a program containing a comment.

```
PROGRAM Yuletide (output);
   (* Prints Christmas and New Year messages *)
BEGIN
   writeln ('Merry Christmas');
   writeln ('Happy New Year')
END.
```

1.5 Errors

The normal sequence of events is that we type a program, compile it and
then run the compiled version. Unfortunately, this does not always work
out in practice. The compiler checks the source program while it is
translating it and, if it detects an error, it refuses to produce a
compiled version of the program. We must attempt to correct the program
and then recompile it. This process may have to be repeated several
times before the program eventually compiles successfully.

The following program contains two errors.

```
PROGRAM CompileErrors (output);
BEGIN
   writln (%Yippee - it works!')
END.
```

The identifier "writeln" has been misspelled as "writln" and a percent
sign has been typed in mistake for a string quote. The compiler will
detect the misspelling of "writeln" and will produce a message to the
effect

         "Identifier not declared"

It should also object to the presence of the percent sign but will
probably not give a very coherent message. Try it on your computer and
see what happens. You may get several messages, possibly finishing with
something like

"Input file exhausted"

which is jargon for

"I've fallen off the end of your program!"

This should be sufficient to convince you that, although the <u>presence</u> of an error may be detected, you may well be left in doubt as to its precise <u>nature</u> and <u>location</u>. To remove these <u>compilation errors</u>, you must correct your program and techniques for changing programs vary from one computer to another.

Even when our program has compiled successfully our problems may not be over because some errors cannot be detected until the program is run. We may have to return to our correct-and-compile cycle (possibly several times) before we get a successful run. With the little Pascal we have covered so far, there is little scope for <u>run-time</u> errors but the following program will serve as an illustration.

```
PROGRAM RunTimeError (output);
BEGIN
    writeln ('This program produces only one line ',
             'of output but it is a very long line ',
             'of output and, in fact, it contains a ',
             'total of 134 characters')
END.
```

It is unlikely that the output device will be able to display 134 characters on one line so the program will be unable to do what it intends. Different computers handle this situation in different ways – see what yours does. It may move on to the next line automatically when one output line is full; it may <u>overprint</u> when it reaches the last character position of the output line (rather like a typewriter with its carriage jammed against a wall); it may abandon execution when the end of the output line is reached and produce a run-time error message.

1.6 Exercises

*1. Write a program to draw a rocket

```
        *
       ***
      *****
      *****
      *****
      *****
     *******
    **       **
```

preceded and followed by a few blank lines. If your terminal has a
visual display, run your program several times in quick succession.
This should give an impression of the rocket travelling up the
screen.

*2. Write a program to print your name and address within a border. Use
any character of your choice for the border.

 3. Write a program to produce a party invitation. The invitation
should include dotted lines for the later addition of name, place,
time etc.

 4. Write a program to draw a Christmas tree with the message 'Merry
Christmas' printed below.

*5. Write a program to print your initials in large letters, something
like this:

```
    L          V     V        AAA
    L          V     V       A   A
    L          V     V      A     A
    L          V     V      AAAAAAA
    L           V   V       A     A
    L            V V        A     A
    LLLLLLL       V         A     A
```

CHAPTER 2
Think of a Number

The previous chapter showed how to write programs to print strings. Most programs print messages of one sort or another and, in addition, process some supplied data. This data is often numeric and this chapter shows how numbers can be introduced to a program.

2.1 Constants

A number is a particular example of a constant and, in Pascal, numbers are of two types: integer and real. Integer constants (with no decimal point) and real constants (with a decimal point) are typed in the conventional mathematical form. Here are some integer constants

        123
        -1
         0
    4623784502
      -7897
        999

and some real constants

        10.0
    -347.8216
      3.14159265358979323746

but some may be beyond the range or accuracy of your computer.

    The largest integer which can be represented is available in the form of a predefined, named constant "maxint". All integers must be in the range +maxint. A typical value of "maxint" is 32767 ($2^{15}-1$).

    On a small computer, the range of reals could be approximately $\pm 10^{40}$ and about seven significant figures might be recorded. In this case, the value of pi given above would be rounded by the computer to 3.141593. As you will probably have guessed, integers and reals are represented differently inside the computer.

    Real numbers written as above are said to be in fixed point form. So that very large, or very small, real values may be expressed conveniently Pascal also offers a floating point notation. A number expressed as a floating point constant has the form

+--+
| |
| aEb |
| |
| where   a is an integer or fixed point real value |
| and   b is an integer |
| |
+--+

The letter "E" is interpreted as "times 10 to the power". Here are some examples of floating point constants and their fixed point equivalents.

```
-3.478216E2  =  -347.8216
       1E-5  =  0.00001
      7.2E9  =  7200000000.0
```

2.2 Expressions

We can process numeric data by using <u>operators</u> and <u>brackets</u> to form
<u>arithmetic</u> <u>expressions</u>. Detailed discussion of expressions will follow
in chapter 3; for the present it will suffice to know that

```
+   represents addition
-   represents subtraction
*   represents multiplication
/   represents (real) division
```

and that operators are applied from left to right at any one bracket
level subject to the fact that

```
* and /  take precedence over  + and -
```

Here are some examples.

```
        5 + 2 * 3  =  11     (integer)
      (5 + 2) * 3  =  21     (integer)
      9.7 - 14.82  =  -5.12  (real)
           10 / 5  =   2.0   (real)
7 + 8.4 / 2.1 * 2  =  15.0   (real)
```

Arithmetic expressions may be supplied as parameters to "writeln"
but, unlike strings, they are not enclosed within string quotes. The

----

```
PROGRAM Box (output);

    (* This program prints the capacity and each of
       the three possibly different flat face areas
       of a box with dimensions 13cm * 7cm * 4cm *)

BEGIN
    writeln ('For a box with the following dimensions :-');
    writeln ('   length: 13 cm    width: 7 cm    depth: 4 cm');
    writeln ('the area of the base is', 13 * 7, ' sq cm');
    writeln ('the area of each side is', 13 * 4, ' sq cm');
    writeln ('the area of each end is', 7 * 4, ' sq cm');
    writeln ('the capacity is', 13 * 7 * 4, ' cc')
END.
```

                        Figure 2.1

----

program of figure 2.1 produces the output shown in figure 2.2. A gap
precedes each computed value because integers are printed in such a way
that they all occupy the same number of character positions. This
predefined <u>field width</u> varies from one computer to another; the above
example assumes an integer field width of 7. Each computer also imposes
a predefined field width upon reals.

```
     For a box with the following dimensions :-
         length: 13 cm    width: 7 cm   depth: 4 cm
     the area of the base is     91 sq cm
     the area of each side is    52 sq cm
     the area of each end is     28 sq cm
     the capacity is     364 cc

                    Figure 2.2
```

2.3 User-defined constants

"maxint" is a named constant. Further named constants may be introduced
by the user. These can make a program more transparent and easier to
modify. A constant <u>declaration</u> has the form

```
         i = c;

   where  i is an identifier
   and    c is a constant
```

Notice that the declaration is followed by a semicolon although, as
mentioned in chapter 1, a semicolon is a separator. Unlike a statement,
a declaration will <u>always</u> be followed by something from which it must be
separated so it is convenient to regard a semicolon as a statement
<u>separator</u> and a declaration <u>terminator.</u> Here are some examples of user-
defined constants.

```
        threenines = 999;
     retirementage = 65;
                pi = 3.14159;
         Fbloodheat = 98.6;
         Cbloodheat = 37;
         tinynumber = 1E-20;
          emergency = threenines;
```

     Constant declarations appear between the PROGRAM line and BEGIN,
heralded by a single occurrence of the reserved word

        CONST

     Figure 2.3 introduces user-defined constants to the program of
figure 2.1.

```
PROGRAM BoxWithUserDefinedConstants (output);

    (* For a box of given dimensions, this program
       prints the capacity and each of the three
       possibly different flat face areas *)

    CONST
        length = 13;   width = 7;   depth = 4;

    BEGIN
        writeln ('For a box with the following dimensions :-');
        writeln ('   length:', length, ' cm   width:', width,
                 ' cm   depth:', depth, ' cm');
        writeln ('the area of the base is',
                     length * width, ' sq cm');
        writeln ('the area of each side is',
                     length * depth, ' sq cm');
        writeln ('the area of each end is',
                     width * depth, ' sq cm');
        writeln ('the capacity is',
                     length * width * depth, ' cc')
    END.
```

                        Figure 2.3

Apart from some spacing, this program produces the same output as
the previous version - but notice the improvements.

Transparency

The relevance of each constant, and hence each expression, is
clearer.

Modification

This program can be applied to a different box more easily than
could the previous version - we merely change the values in the
constant definitions. In the previous program we would have to scan
the entire program and change every occurrence of each constant.
The improved program is not only easier to modify, it is safer - we
have less chance of making a mistake when making the changes.

Figure 2.4 shows another example.

2.4 Formatted output

The standard field widths imposed upon output values can be overridden.
A field width can be specified for any parameter of "write" or
"writeln". If the field is too wide, the output is right-justified and
the field space-filled from the left. If the field width specified for
an arithmetic value is too small, it is ignored and the minimum field

----

```
PROGRAM Circle (output);

    (* Computes the diameter and area
       of a circle of given radius *)

  CONST
      pi = 3.14159;
      radius = 2.1;

BEGIN
    writeln ('A circle of radius', radius, ' cm');
    writeln ('has diameter', 2 * radius, ' cm ',
             'and area', pi * radius * radius, ' sq cm')
END.
```

                        Figure 2.4

----

width necessary is used. So, if we supply a field width of 1 for an integer, no additional spaces will be output.

   The field width follows the parameter and the two are separated by a colon. Real values are printed in floating point form unless a second format parameter is specified. This follows the first, separated from it by a colon, and dictates the number of decimal places that will appear in the output. The three statements

```
        writeln ('*', 7:1, ' ':6, 423:1, 6:5);
        writeln ('*', 49:8, 'Fred':9);
        writeln ('*', 5.6789:5:2, ' ', 7458.13:7)
```

produce the following output

```
        *7      423     6
        *        49     Fred
        * 5.68 7.46E03
```

```
PROGRAM Dollars (output);

    (* Prints three dollar signs *)

  CONST
      n = 5;

BEGIN
    writeln ('$', '$' :n+1, '$' :2*n+1)
END.
```

                        Figure 2.5

In the "Box" program of figure 2.3 we could follow each of the
expressions "length*width", "length*depth", "width*depth" and
"length*width*depth" by the format specification ":1". We should then
include an extra space at the end of each string preceding these
expressions for otherwise the computer will print no spaces between the
string and the value.

In these examples the format parameters have been integer constants
but they may be any integer expressions. The program of figure 2.5
prints three dollar signs. The first two are separated by n spaces,
where "n" is a user-defined constant, and the second and third are
separated by 2n spaces.

2.5 Variables

A constant declaration associates an identifier with a value of some
particular type. This binding is permanent: the value associated cannot
be changed. A _variable_ is an identifier which may be associated with
different values (but all of the same type) at different times during
the execution of a program. Variable declarations have the form

---

$i_1, i_2, ..., i_n : t;$

where $i_1, i_2, ..., i_n$ are identifiers

and   t is a _type_

For the present we restrict our attention to the types "integer" and
"real". For reasons which will become apparent later, these are said to
be _scalar_ types and "integer" is known also as an _ordinal_ type. We use
integer variables for things which can only be whole numbers and reals
for things which may be fractional. Here are some examples of variable
declarations.

```
            age : integer;
   noofchildren : integer;
     heightinmm : integer;
     rateofflow : real;
      hourlypay : real;
```

If these five declarations were to appear consecutively in one program,
they would normally be written in the following form.

```
   age, noofchildren, heightinmm : integer;
   rateofflow, hourlypay : real;
```

Variable declarations appear between the constant declarations (if there
are any) and BEGIN, heralded by a single occurrence of the reserved word

```
   VAR
```

We can think of a variable as a box (or storage location) inside
the computer, with a name stuck on. When we declare a variable we
specify the shape of the box (by quoting the type) and the name we want

sticking on (by quoting an identifier). The five declarations above can
be pictured as follows.

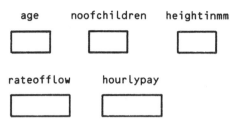

ALL boxes which are to hold integers will be the same shape. ALL boxes
which are to hold reals will be the same shape - but not the same shape
as integer boxes.

2.6 Input

A variable declaration introduces a variable but associates no value
with it - its value is said to be <u>undefined</u>. One way of giving a value
to a variable is to type a value when the program is running and make
the program give this value to the variable. We then say the program
<u>reads</u> the value.

So far, program data (that is, each initial value) has been
supplied at compile-time via constant declarations (eg "length", "width"
and "depth" in figure 2.3). It is often preferable to supply data at
run-time. This has the advantage that different runs of one program can
utilise different data; there is no need to change the program.

If a program is to read a value from the terminal, the identifier
"input" must appear in the PROGRAM line along with "output", the two
being separated by a comma.

PROGRAM ... (input, output);

In Pascal, reading can be achieved by either of two statements: "read"
and "readln".

2.6.1 <u>read</u>

A read-statement has the form

read $(v_1, v_2, ..., v_n)$

where $v_1, v_2, ..., v_n$ are variables,
possibly of different types

When the statement is encountered at run-time, program execution halts
until data is supplied. The user must then type one value for each
variable in the list. These values will be assigned to the variables in

the order in which they appear within the read-statement. Each number
typed must be terminated by some character which cannot be part of the
number - usually this is either a space or end-of-line. Any additional
spaces or ends of lines which precede a number will be ignored.

     The program of figure 2.6 reads a person's age and states the age
after the next birthday. When this program is run nothing will happen
until the user types an integer. The program will then respond with the
appropriate output. This illustrates the reading process but it also
indicates the need for an improvement in the program.

```
PROGRAM NextYearsAge (input, output);

    (* Increments a supplied age by 1 *)

VAR
    agenow : integer;

BEGIN
    read (agenow);
    writeln ('Age after next birthday will be ', agenow + 1)
END.
```

Figure 2.6

We should never allow the situation where the program has halted
awaiting input when we might not be expecting it.

```
If your program wants you to type something -
   make sure it tells you what it wants!
```

So we should precede the read-statement of figure 2.6 by a write-
statement. The program should be as in figure 2.7. The write-statement
is obeyed before the read-statement is encountered and we say the
program prompts the user to type something. Because the prompt is issued
by "write", the user will be asked to type the value on the same line.
If "writeln" were used instead, the typed data would appear on the next
line.

     Prompting is particularly important when several values are to be
read - the user must be told the order in which to type them. If our
"Box" program of figure 2.3 were modified to read the dimensions, it
might include the read-statement

```
read (length, width, depth)
```

preceded by statements to produce a suitable prompt:

```
writeln ('Please supply the dimensions of your box');
writeln ('(in cm) in the order length, width, depth');
```

```
PROGRAM NextYearsAgeWithPrompt (input, output);

    (* Increments a supplied age by 1 *)

  VAR
    agenow : integer;

BEGIN
  write ('How old are you? ');   read (agenow);
  writeln ('After your next birthday you will be ', agenow + 1)
END.
```

Figure 2.7

Perhaps better is the program of figure 2.8 which generates a separate
prompt for each dimension. Notice that the program no longer prints the
dimensions of the box. Because these are now typed by the user when the
program is running, they are there to be seen.

Program output is usually <u>buffered</u>. Output generated by successive
write-statements sits in a buffer until a writeln-statement is obeyed. A

```
PROGRAM BoxWithRead (input, output);

    (* For a box of given dimensions, this program
       prints the capacity and each of the three
       possibly different flat face areas *)

  VAR
    length, width, depth : integer;

BEGIN
  writeln ('Please supply the dimensions of your box (in cm)');
  write ('   length: ');   read (length);
  write ('    width: ');   read (width);
  write ('    depth: ');   read (depth);
  writeln;

  writeln ('The area of the base is ',
                    length * width :1, ' sq cm');
  writeln ('The area of each side is ',
                    length * depth :1, ' sq cm');
  writeln ('The area of each end is ',
                    width * depth :1, ' sq cm');
  writeln ('The capacity is ',
                length * width * depth :1, ' cc')
END.
```

Figure 2.8

---

good terminal implementation will print any information currently in the
output buffer when reading is encountered and the behaviour of the
programs of figures 2.7 and 2.8 will be sensible only if such an
implementation is available. Unfortunately, some implementations refuse
to empty the output buffer until a writeln-statement is obeyed. If you
find yourself with such an implementation you will have to issue prompts
with writeln-statements, and not write-statements. You could also
approach your supplier and request an improvement!

2.6.2 readln

"readln" is to "read" as "writeln" is to "write". The form is the same
except that no parameter need be supplied. The effect of

        readln

is to terminate the current line of input. This means that nothing
further is read from the line; any further characters, up to and
including the end-of-line character, are skipped.

    When "readln" is supplied with parameters

        readln (a, b, ..., c)

is equivalent to

        read (a, b, ..., c);   readln

    The program of figure 2.9 accumulates the total stock in a pet shop
which offers four different types of pet. Each number is read from a
different line and anything typed after the number is ignored. The data
could be typed in the form

          7 cats
          4 dogs
        128 rabbits
          1 cannibal fish

and only the numbers would be read.

    Input from a terminal is usually buffer-driven. The information you
type will sit in a buffer until you supply an end-of-line character
(usually called "return" on the terminal keyboard). Consequently, there
will usually be an end-of-line character after each sequence of values
you type as input. We shall therefore use "readln" in preference to
"read" whenever a number (or series of numbers) is to be read and it is
to be expected that the number (or series of numbers) will be followed
by an end-of-line character. This is the case for the dimensions in our
"Box" program and so each could be read by "readln".

    Also, we shall see later that "readln" can be particularly useful
when data is processed on a character-by-character basis rather than in
the form of numbers.

    As a final point, it must be noted that, when "readln" is used, not

all terminal implementations of Pascal behave as described here. To
achieve the effects described above, you may find that you have to type
an extra end-of-line character after each group of values read by a
readln-statement. This should not be so! If your implementation makes
this imposition, consult your supplier and request rectification. The
problem is not serious when integers or reals are being read but it can
wreak havoc when you try the character processing examples of chapter 5.

```
PROGRAM PetShop (input, output);

      (* Sums four integers typed one per line,
         each possibly followed by text *)

   VAR
      pet1s, pet2s, pet3s, pet4s : integer;

BEGIN
   writeln ('Type the number in stock of ',
            'each of your four species');
   writeln (' - one per line');

   readln (pet1s);    readln (pet2s);
   readln (pet3s);    readln (pet4s);

   writeln ('Total number of pets in stock is ',
            pet1s + pet2s + pet3s + pet4s :1)
END.
```

                   Figure 2.9

2.7 Exercises

*1. Write a program to print your computer's value of maxint.

For exercises 2 to 9, supply any required values as user-defined constants at the head of the program.

*2. Charlie is looking forward to his retirement when he reaches 65 but cannot work out when that will be. Write a program that will tell Charlie how many years he has to wait if he supplies his age.

3. Write a program which prints the number of electricity units used if the present and previous meter readings are supplied.

*4. Tom, Dick and Harry want to know their average age. Write a program which will tell them if they supply their ages.

5. Write a program to convert a length in yards, feet and inches to inches.

6. Write a program to compute the perimeter and area of a rectangular field of given length and breadth.

*7. When Charlie does retire, he will be entitiled to an annual pension of one fiftieth of his salary for each complete year's service with his company. Write a program which will tell Charlie what his annual pension will be if he supplies his annual salary and the number of years he has served.

*8. Write a program which will print a payslip for Charlie telling him his gross pay. Charlie is to supply his hourly rate of pay, the number of standard-rate hours he has worked and the number of overtime hours. His overtime rate is 'time and a half', that is, 1.5 times his standard rate.

*9. Four dots are to be printed on the same line. The first dot is to be at the extreme left hand side of the output screen (or page) and is to be separated from the second dot by a specified number of spaces. The gap between the second and third dots is to be two spaces less than that between the first two and the gap between the third and fourth dots two spaces less again.
    Write a program which uses formatted output to produce these dots assuming that the number of spaces in the first gap is small but not less than 4.

*10. Modify your programs for exercises 2 to 9 so that data is read at run-time.

CHAPTER 3
Doing Arithmetic

The last chapter showed how values can be read at run-time and given to variables and also outlined arithmetic expressions. In this chapter we examine expressions in more detail but, first, we see how an expression can be used to assign a value to a variable.

3.1 Assignment statement

A value may be assigned to a variable by an <u>assignment statement</u>. This has the form

```
        v := e

where   v is a variable,
        e is an expression
and     := is the assignment operator
```

The assignment operator is read as 'becomes'. e may have type integer if v has type real but otherwise v and e must have the same type.

When an assignment statement is obeyed the expression on the right hand side is evaluated and the resultant value assigned to the variable on the left. Any value previously associated with the variable is lost (the technical term is <u>overwritten</u>). A variable retains a value assigned to it until it subsequently acquires a different value, either by reading or by direct assignment. For example, a program containing the declarations

```
        CONST
            votingage = 18;
        VAR
            age : integer;
```

might contain the statement

```
        age := votingage - 2
```

Expressions may include variables in the same way that they can include constants. When a variable is encountered within an expression at run-time the current value of the variable is used. Any reference to an undefined value constitutes an error.

We return, yet again, to our "Box" program and notice that, in figure 2.8, the expression

```
        length * width
```

appears twice but must produce the same value each time because the values of "length" and "width" do not change. We can avoid this

---

```
PROGRAM Box (input, output);

    (* For a box of given dimensions, this program
       prints the capacity and each of the three
       possibly different flat face areas *)

    VAR
        length, width, depth, basearea : integer;
BEGIN
    writeln ('Please supply the dimensions of your box (in cm)');
    write ('    length: ');    read (length);
    write ('    width: ');     read (width);
    write ('    depth: ');     read (depth);
    writeln;

    basearea := length * width;

    writeln ('The area of the base is ',
                        basearea :1, ' sq cm');
    writeln ('The area of each side is ',
                    length * depth :1, ' sq cm');
    writeln ('The area of each end is ',
                     width * depth :1, ' sq cm');
    writeln ('The capacity is ',
                    basearea * depth :1, ' cc')
END.
```

Figure 3.1

---

duplication by computing the value of the product once, storing it in a variable and referring to the variable whenever we need to retrieve it. We do this in the program of figure 3.1. Notice that this also makes the program more transparent. The identifier "basearea" conveys more immediate information than does the expression "length * width".

The program of figure 3.2 computes the average and the differences from the average of votes gained by three candidates in an election. Notice that, although the votes are integers, all the variables are real because the average of three integers is not, in general, an integer.

More than one assignment may be made to the same variable. Also, a variable may appear on both the left hand side and the right hand side of the same assignment statement. Both these points are illustrated by the program of figure 3.3 which prints a number and its three successors together with their squares and reciprocals.

To stress the dynamic nature of the assignment statement, consider a section of program to interchange the values of two integer variables "first" and "second". Initially, look at

```
first := second;    second := first
```

```
PROGRAM TomDickandHarry (input, output);

    (* Computes the differences from the
       average of three supplied vote totals *)

  VAR
      tomsvotes, dicksvotes, harrysvotes : integer;
      averagevote, tomsdiff, dicksdiff, harrysdiff : real;
BEGIN
      writeln ('State the number of votes cast for');
      writeln ('     Tom : ');    readln (tomsvotes);
      writeln ('    Dick : ');    readln (dicksvotes);
      writeln ('   Harry : ');    readln (harrysvotes);

      averagevote := (tomsvotes + dicksvotes + harrysvotes) / 3;
      writeln ('The average of the votes is ', averagevote :6:1);

      tomsdiff := tomsvotes - averagevote;
      dicksdiff := dicksvotes - averagevote;
      harrysdiff := harrysvotes - averagevote;

      writeln ('Votes gained differ from the average as follows');
      writeln ('    Tom:  ', tomsdiff :6:1,
               '    Dick: ', dicksdiff :6:1,
               '    Harry:', harrysdiff :6:1)
END.
```

Figure 3.2

Does this work? Well, let's see - suppose "first" has the value 26 and "second" the value 47.

```
    first      second
   ┌──────┐   ┌──────┐
   │  26  │   │  47  │
   └──────┘   └──────┘
```

When the assignment

        first := second

is obeyed the value of "second" remains unchanged and "first" takes the value of "second" (47).

```
    first      second
   ┌──────┐   ┌──────┐
   │  47  │   │  47  │
   └──────┘   └──────┘
```

Now, when the assignment

        second := first

```
PROGRAM SquaresAndReciprocals (input, output);

    (* Prints four consecutive integers together
       with their squares and reciprocals *)

    VAR
        n : integer;

BEGIN
    write ('What is the starting value? ');
    readln (n);

    writeln;
    writeln ('        2');
    writeln ('  n     n     1/n');
    writeln (n :4, n*n :6, 1/n :8:3);

    n := n + 1;
    writeln (n :4, n*n :6, 1/n :8:3);

    n := n + 1;
    writeln (n :4, n*n :6, 1/n :8:3);

    n := n + 1;
    writeln (n :4, n*n :6, 1/n :8:3)
END.
```

Figure 3.3

---

is obeyed the value of "first" remains unchanged and "second" takes the value of "first" (47).

first   second

```
┌──────┐     ┌──────┐
│  47  │     │  47  │
└──────┘     └──────┘
```

So, the answer is "No - this does not work"! You might like to try reordering the assignments - it doesn't help! What are we doing wrong?

The trouble is that, as soon as the assignment

        first := second

has been obeyed, all record of the previous value of "first" (26) has been lost. So, in order to give this value to "second" after we have changed the value of "first", we must store this previous value of "first" - hence, we need another variable (say, "oldfirst") to hold the old value of "first" temporarily. Now we can achieve the interchange using three (not two) assignments.

        oldfirst := first;   first := second;   second := oldfirst

Let us make sure this works for first = 26 and second = 47.

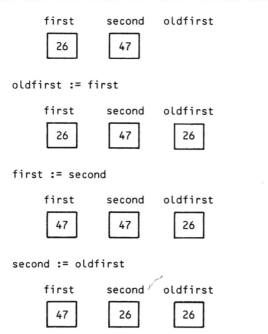

oldfirst := first

first := second

second := oldfirst

Hooray!

The sequence

    oldsecond := second;   second := first;   first := oldsecond

works equally well.

3.2 Arithmetic expressions

3.2.1 Arithmetic operators

The operators +, -, * and / are applicable to integer and real operands. When applied to two operands, the result of an addition (+), subtraction (-) or multiplication (*) is of type real if either of its operands has type real; it is of type integer only if <u>both</u> its operands have type integer. The result of a real division (/) is always of type real. The operators + and - may be applied to a single operand. The operator - then acts as negation and + has no effect.

    There are two operators which are applicable only to two integer operands and each produces an integer result.

```
DIV  -  integer division
           (gives the integer part of division)
```

```
MOD  -  modulo reduction
           (gives the remainder left by integer division)
```

The first operand should be positive or zero and the second should be positive. Here are some examples.

```
15 DIV 7  = 2        15 MOD 7  = 1
 7 DIV 15 = 0         7 MOD 15 = 7
15 DIV 5  = 3        15 MOD 5  = 0
 5 DIV 15 = 0         5 MOD 15 = 5
 6 DIV 6  = 1         6 MOD 6  = 0
```

The program of figure 3.4 takes a 3-digit integer, introduced as a user-defined constant, and prints it backwards.

DIV and MOD have the same precedence as * and /. The brackets "(" and ")" may be used to override the precedence rules. At any one bracket level operators are applied from left to right subject to the fact that multiplying operators {* / DIV MOD} are applied before adding operators {+ -}. Thus, in figure 3.4, the brackets of (n MOD 100) are superfluous but their inclusion perhaps aids transparency.

```
PROGRAM ReverseInt (output);

        (* Reverses a positive three digit integer,
           specified as a user-defined constant *)

    CONST
        n = 472;

    VAR
        hundreds, tens, units : integer;

BEGIN
    hundreds := n DIV 100;
    tens     := (n MOD 100) DIV 10;
    units    := n MOD 10;

    writeln (n, ' reversed is ', units :1, tens :1, hundreds :1)
END.
```

Figure 3.4

3.2.2 Standard functions

Pascal provides a number of standard functions to perform certain frequently required computations. Each must be supplied with one parameter and produces a result of some specified type. The parameter is bracketed and follows the function name. The parameter may be any

expression of the appropriate type. A function may be used anywhere in
an expression where a variable or constant of the same type could be
used.

There are six functions which are applicable only to real operands
and each produces a real result.

```
arctan  -  arc tangent
cos     -  cosine
exp     -  exponential
ln      -  natural logarithm
sin     -  sine
sqrt    -  square root
```

The program of figure 3.5 computes the roots of a quadratic
equation

$$ax^2 + bx + c = 0$$

assuming the equation has real roots. It uses the well-known formula

$$x = \frac{-b \pm \sqrt{b^2 - 4ac}}{2a}$$

```
PROGRAM QuadEqnWithRealRoots (input, output);

        (* Computes the roots of a quadratic equation
           on the assumption that the roots are real *)
    VAR
        a, b, c : integer;
        x1, x2, rootofdisc : real;
BEGIN
    writeln ('Please type the coefficients of your equation');
    writeln ('  in the order:  x squared, x, constant');
    readln (a, b, c);

    rootofdisc := sqrt (b*b - 4*a*c);
    x1 := (-b + rootofdisc) / (2*a);
    x2 := (-b - rootofdisc) / (2*a);

    writeln ('The two roots are ', x1 :6:2, ' and ', x2 :6:2)
END.
```

Figure 3.5

Of course, this program will not work if the equation does not have real
roots. The discriminant (b*b-4*a*c) will then be negative and so an
execution error will be flagged when an attempt is made to evaluate its
square root.

Some programming languages provide an exponentiation operator to raise any positive number to any power. This is an expensive operation involving the application of the functions "exp" and "ln". Pascal (purposely) does not provide such an operator - the functions "exp" and "ln" must be applied explicitly if required. The expression

        exp (b * ln(a))

gives the value of "a" raised to the power "b".

The trigonometric functions "sin" and "cos" must be supplied with an angle expressed in radians, not degrees, and the result delivered by "arctan" is in radians, not degrees. The program of figure 3.6 accepts an angle expressed in degrees and prints its tangent. Then, purely to illustrate the use of "arctan", it converts the computed value back into an angle quoted in degrees.

```
PROGRAM ToTanAndBack (input, output);

    (* Computes the tangent of an angle, supplied in degrees,
       and then reconstructs the angle from its tangent *)

CONST
  pi = 3.14159;

VAR
  angle, angleinrads, tangent, toradians : real;

BEGIN
  write ('Give me an angle in degrees ');    readln (angle);
  toradians := pi / 180;
  angleinrads := angle * toradians;
  tangent := sin (angleinrads) / cos (angleinrads);
  writeln ('Its tangent is ', tangent);
  writeln ('Conversion back to an angle in degrees gives ',
          arctan (tangent) / toradians)
END.
```

Figure 3.6

This program introduces "pi" as a user-defined constant. If you wish to compute "pi" to the maximum accuracy of your machine you can use "arctan":

        pi := 4 * arctan(1)

There are two functions which can supply an integer or a real result, depending upon the type of parameter supplied.

```
abs  -  absolute magnitude
sqr  -  square
```

In the quadratic equation example of figure 3.5 the discriminant can be
written in the form

        sqr (b) - 4 * a * c

The function "sqr" should always be used when the item to be squared is
an expression more complicated than a single constant or variable.

    Recall that a real value cannot be assigned to an integer variable.
Consequently two functions are provided to map a real value onto an
integer.

---

        round - rounds to the nearest integer
        trunc - rounds towards zero

Here are some examples of "trunc".

            trunc (7.4) = 7   trunc (-7.4) = -7
            trunc (7.5) = 7   trunc (-7.5) = -7
            trunc (7.6) = 7   trunc (-7.6) = -7

"round(x)" is defined to be

            trunc (x + 0.5)   for x $\geq$ 0

            trunc (x - 0.5)   for x < 0

Here are some examples of "round".

            round (7.4) = 7   round (-7.4) = -7
            round (7.5) = 8   round (-7.5) = -8
            round (7.6) = 8   round (-7.6) = -8

3.2.3 Precision of reals

Within the computer, integers are stored exactly but reals involve some
inherent error. This is because only a certain number of significant
figures can be stored. A computer stores values in binary but we can
illustrate the problem using decimal.

    Suppose we have a decimal machine capable of storing   four
significant figures. The expression

        1/3

evaluated to four significant figures is

        0.3333

The expression

        2 * (1 / 3)

therefore produces

0.6666

The expression

2 / 3

evaluated to four significant figures is

0.6667

So, two expressions which are mathematically equivalent can produce different values. Alternatively, two expressions which are not mathematically equivalent can produce the same value. Consider the following difference of two terms:

2 * 500.7 - (700 + 300.6)

Mathematically this is

1001.4 - 1000.6

which is 0.8. To our decimal computer, however, the two terms appear the same. Both 1001.4 and 1000.6, when rounded to four significant figures, are 1001. Our computer, evaluating the original expression, will therefore produce 0 rather than 0.8.

Fortunately, the number of significant binary digits stored by your computer should be equivalent to more than four decimal digits. The significance is typically between seven decimal digits for a small computer to fourteen for a large one. The representational errors inherent in real numbers are therefore less than those indicated in the examples above but, as computation proceeds, these errors accumulate. Be on your guard!

If you are likely to become involved with large numerical calculations, you should consult a book which deals specifically with numerical computation. "An Introduction to Numerical Methods with Pascal", written by L V Atkinson and P J Harley and published by Addison-Wesley, is such a book.

3.3 Exercises

*1. The first two terms of the "Fibonacci Sequence" are 0 and 1 and each successive term is the sum of the previous two. Thus the sequence starts 0, 1, 1, 2, 3, 5, 8, ... Write a program which, given two consecutive Fibonacci numbers, produces the next three.

2. Write a program which will print the net price of an item, the tax payable on the item and the total cost of the item. The net price and the tax percentage are each quoted as an integer.

*3. A pay rise of 9.4% has been awarded to a company's employees and is to be backdated for 5 months. Write a program which will accept an annual salary and will print the salary increase, the new annual salary, the new monthly pay and the amount of backdated pay due.

4. A capital invested and the interest rates for each of three successive years are supplied. Interest is calculated at the end of each year and added to the current sum invested. Write a program to print the original sum, the interest awarded each year and the total investment at the end of the three years.

*5. Write a program to convert a Fahrenheit temperature to Centigrade.

6.   "As I was going to St. Ives,
       I met a man with seven wives.
       Each wife had seven sacks;
       Each sack had seven cats;
       Each cat had seven kits.
       Kits, cats, sacks, wives;
       How many were going to St. Ives?"

   The classical answer to this is
          "One; all the other travellers were leaving St. Ives!"
   Despite this, assume that all were travelling in the same direction and write a program which answers the question and also itemizes the number of people, the number of sacks and the number of animals.

7. A secret service organisation uses numeric codes for agents and cities. When agent a is to go to city c a coded message is sent to central intelligence. Instead of referring to the agent and the destination directly the message incorporates the two values $a-c$ and a^2-c^2. Write a decoding program which, given these two coded values, deduces which agent and city are involved.

*8. Carol wishes to lay one course of carpet tiles across her bedroom. Assuming the width of her bedroom and the width of a carpet tile are specified as an integral number of centimetres, write a program to tell Carol how much she will have to discard from the last tile to be laid.

*9. Write a program to produce change from $1 for any purchase less than $1 but a whole number of cents. The program is to indicate which coins are to be paid and should minimise the number of coins. Denominations available are 50c, 10c, 5c, 2c and 1c.

10. Using a 24-hour clock a time can be represented by an integer in the range 0 (midnight) through 1200 (noon) to 2359 (11.59 pm). Write a program to add a given duration, expressed in hours and minutes, to a specified time.

*11. Write a program to determine the length of the hypotenuse of a right-angled triangle, given the lengths of the other two sides.

12. Write a program to compute the area of a triangle using the fact that, for a triangle with sides of length a, b and c, the area is given by

$$\sqrt{s(s-a)(s-b)(s-c)}$$

where

$$s = \frac{a + b + c}{2}$$

13. If a cubic equation

$$ax^3 + bx^2 + cx + d = 0$$

has two complex roots and one real root, the real root (say u) may be found by Cardano's method:

$$u = s - p/3s - r/3$$

where

$$s = \sqrt[3]{(t - q)/2}$$

$$t = (4p^3 + 27q^2)/27$$

$$q = d/a - cr/3a + 2r^3/27$$

$$p = c/a - r^2/3$$

and $r = b/a$

If a cubic equation has three distinct real roots then t<0 and Cardano's method cannot be applied without resorting to complex arithmetic.

Write a program to apply Cardano's method to find the real root of a cubic equation of the appropriate kind. Test your program on each of the following equations

$$4x^3 - 12x^2 + x - 3 = 0$$

$$x^3 - 7x^2 + 4x - 28 = 0$$

CHAPTER 4
Being Choosy

In each program considered so far, every statement is obeyed once, and once only, when the program is executed. This is not the case with most realistic programs. Computers have the ability to make simple tests and we can make the execution of some statements conditional upon the outcome of these tests. There are two aspects to this. We can achieve selection (some statements are obeyed and some are not) and repetition (a group of statements is executed repeatedly - this is called looping). Loops are discussed in Chapters 6 and 7; in this chapter we concentrate on selection.

4.1 If-statement

The if-statement exists in a full and a shortened form. The full form is

```
        IF t THEN s1 ELSE s2

    where  t is a test
    and    s1 and s2 are any statements
```

Notice that no semicolons appear within the if-statement but a semicolon will follow the if-statement (that is, after s2) if the if-statement is followed by another statement.

When the statement is encountered at run-time the test t is made. If the test holds then s1 is obeyed (and s2 is not); if the test does not hold then s2 is obeyed (and s1 is not). In either case control then passes to the statement next in sequence after the if-statement.

Tests can include the relational operators

```
    <    less than
    <=   less than or equal to
    >    greater than
    >=   greater than or equal to
    =    equal to
    <>   not equal to
```

and these have the lowest precedence of all the operators.

If "a" and "b" are two integer variables with different values, the following if-statement prints their values in ascending order.

```
        IF a<b THEN
            writeln (a, b)
        ELSE
            writeln (b, a)
```

The computation performed by the standard function "abs" can be described by an if-statement. The assignment

        y := abs(x)

is equivalent to

        IF x >= 0 THEN
            y := x
        ELSE
            y := -x

Rather than choose which of two statements to obey we often wish to make a simpler decision - whether to obey one statement or not. An abbreviated form of the if-statement is available for this.

```
              IF t THEN s

        where  t is a test
        and    s is any statement
```

If the test t holds, s is obeyed; if not, s is not obeyed. In either case control passes to the statement next in sequence after the if-statement. This form is illustrated in the program of figure 4.1 which reads a bank balance and a withdrawal and computes the new balance.

```
        PROGRAM BankBalance (input, output);

              (* Reads a balance and a withdrawal
                 and updates the balance *)

          VAR
              balance, withdrawal : real;

        BEGIN
            write ('What is your current balance? $');
            readln (balance);

            write ('How much do you wish to withdraw? $');
            readln (withdrawal);

            balance := balance - withdrawal;
            writeln ('Your new balance is $', balance :4:2);

            IF balance < 0 THEN
                writeln ('Your account is overdrawn -',
                         ' please see the manager!')
          END.

                        Figure 4.1
```

```
PROGRAM MinOfThreeInts (input, output);

    (* Determines the smallest of three integers *)

   VAR
      n1, n2, n3, min : integer;

BEGIN
   write ('Type three integers ');
   readln (n1, n2, n3);

   IF n1 < n2 THEN
      min := n1
   ELSE
      min := n2;

   IF n3 < min THEN
      min := n3;

   writeln ('The smallest of these is ', min :1)
END.
```

Figure 4.2

The program of figure 4.2 includes both forms of if-statement. It determines the smallest of three supplied integers. Two of the integers are compared and the smaller of these assigned to a variable "min"; this entails a two-way choice and so uses a full if-statement. The third value is then compared with this current minimum and the value of "min" changed only if the third value is smaller; this is achieved with a reduced if-statement.

4.2 Case-statement

An if-statement provides a two-way selection based on a two-way test. A case-statement extends this notion to a multi-way choice based on a range of values. The usual form is

```
        CASE e OF
          v_1 : s_1;
          v_2 : s_2;

           . . .

          v_n : s_n
        END (* CASE *)

    where  e is an expression of some ordinal type, say t,
           v_1, v_2, ..., v_n  are distinct constants of type t
    and    s_1, s_2, ..., s_n  are statements
```

The only ordinal type we have met is "integer" so, for the present, we must take "t" to be "integer".

At run-time, only one of the limbs s_1, s_2, ..., s_n will be obeyed. The selector e is evaluated and, assuming it produces one of the values v_1, v_2, ..., v_n, the statement labelled with the appropriate value is selected. The selector must evaluate to one of the supplied case labels; failure to do so constitutes an error.

> Use of a case statement is appropriate when
> selection is governed by an ordinal expression
> whose values are few and known.

The program of figure 4.3 uses a case-statement to print the 'name' of a supplied digit. It also illustrates a combination of "write" and "writeln". A line of output text is built up by a write-statement at one point in the program and a writeln-statement at another.

```
PROGRAM DigitNamer (input, output);

    (* Names a supplied digit *)

    VAR
        digit : integer;
BEGIN
    write ('Give me a digit ');    readln (digit);
    write ('This is ');
    CASE digit OF
        0 : writeln ('zero');
        1 : writeln ('one');
        2 : writeln ('two');
        3 : writeln ('three');
        4 : writeln ('four');
        5 : writeln ('five');
        6 : writeln ('six');
        7 : writeln ('seven');
        8 : writeln ('eight');
        9 : writeln ('nine')
    END (* CASE *)
END.
```

Figure 4.3

In this example the case labels form a contiguous sequence but this need not be the case. A case-statement to name a prime digit would have the form

```
CASE digit OF
   1 : writeln ('one');
   2 : writeln ('two');
   3 : writeln ('three');
   5 : writeln ('five');
   7 : writeln ('seven')
END (* CASE *)
```

The selector here is an integer variable but it can be a more complicated expression. We illustrate this with a program to determine which quadrant contains a supplied angle, specified in degrees. The four quadrants are defined as follows for angles less than 360 degrees.

```
 first :    0 <=  angle <    90
second :   90 <=  angle <   180
 third :  180 <=  angle <   270
fourth :  270 <=  angle <   360
```

Any angle in excess of 360 degrees is equivalent to an angle 360 degrees smaller. The program is in figure 4.4.

```
PROGRAM Quadrants (input, output);

        (* Determines the quadrant occupied
           by a supplied angle.  The angle
           is assumed not to be negative *)

    VAR
        angle : real;

BEGIN
    write ('Give me an angle in degrees ');
    readln (angle);

    write ('It lies in the ');

    CASE (trunc(angle) MOD 360) DIV 90 OF
       0 : write ('first');
       1 : write ('second');
       2 : write ('third');
       3 : write ('fourth')
    END (* CASE *);

    writeln (' quadrant')
END.
```

Figure 4.4

One case limb may be prefixed by more than one case-label. The program of figure 4.5 illustrates this. It states an insurance group applicable for a specified age. The insurance company involved has four groups corresponding to the following age ranges.

```
              Group A :  15 - 19
              Group B :  20 - 29
              Group C :  30 - 49
              Group D :  50 - 64
```

A case limb may be empty. The insurance grouping program will fail
if it is supplied with an integer less than 15. We can make it accept an
integer in the range 0 to 14 by including a limb prefixed with the
values 0, 1 and 2. We should arrange for this limb to print some
suitable message but, if we wish, we can make it do nothing at all by
making it an empty limb:

```
              CASE age DIV 5 OF
                 0, 1, 2   : ;
                 3         : writeln ('A');
                 4, 5      : writeln ('B');
                 6, 7, 8, 9 : writeln ('C');
                10,11,12   : writeln ('D')
              END (* CASE *)
```

Notice that the semicolon is necessary to separate the empty limb from
the case label 3 which heralds the next limb. If the last limb is empty
it need not be followed by a semicolon, but a semicolon must separate it
from its preceding limb.

```
              CASE age DIV 5 OF
                 3         : writeln ('A');
                 4, 5      : writeln ('B');
                 6, 7, 8, 9 : writeln ('C');
                10,11,12   : writeln ('D');
                 0, 1, 2   :
              END (* CASE *)
```

```
      PROGRAM InsuranceGrouping (input, output);

              (* Categorizes an age into one of four groups }

          VAR
              age : integer;

      BEGIN
          write ('Supply an age ');   readln (age);
          write ('Insurance group is ');
          CASE age DIV 5 OF
             3         : writeln ('A');
             4, 5      : writeln ('B');
             6, 7, 8, 9 : writeln ('C');
            10,11,12   : writeln ('D')
          END (* CASE *)
      END.
```

                         Figure 4.5

The ordering of case limbs is immaterial but to aid program transparency they should, as in these examples, appear in a sensible order.

As a final note on case-statements it must be mentioned that the storage required is usually dependent upon the range of the case labels. Consequently, a case-statement may not be the best construct to use if the range of labels is large but the number of limbs is few.

4.3 Compound statement

Only one statement may be supplied as a case limb or following THEN or ELSE but we often wish to supply more than one. Pascal provides a means of bracketing statements together so that they become one compound statement. BEGIN and END are used as statement brackets.

Recall the quadratic equation example of figure 3.5. It assumed that the equation had real roots. We can improve the program by checking for this - a quadratic equation has complex roots if the discriminant, sqr(b)-4*a*c, is negative. The program of figure 4.6 makes this check.

Better still, we can compute the roots even if they are complex. The computer knows nothing of complex numbers but we can compute the

---

```
PROGRAM QuadEqnWithCheck (input, output);

        (* Determines whether the roots of a quadratic
           equation are real or complex and computes the
           roots if they are real *)

    VAR
        a, b, c, disc : integer;
        x1, x2, rootofdisc : real;

BEGIN
    writeln ('Give the coefficients of the equation');
    readln (a, b, c);

    disc := sqr(b) - 4*a*c;

    IF disc >= 0 THEN
    BEGIN
        rootofdisc := sqrt (disc);
        x1 := (-b + rootofdisc) / (2*a);
        x2 := (-b - rootofdisc) / (2*a);
        writeln ('Roots are ', x1 :6:2, ' and ', x2 :6:2)
    END ELSE
        writeln ('Equation has complex roots')
END.
```

Figure 4.6

```
    PROGRAM QuadEqn (input, output);

        (* Computes the roots of a quadratic equation,
           whether they are real or complex *)

    VAR
        a, b, c, disc : integer;
        x1, x2, realpart, imagpart, rootofdisc : real;
BEGIN
    writeln ('Give the coefficients of the equation');
    readln (a, b, c);

    disc := sqr(b) - 4*a*c;

    IF disc >= 0 THEN
    BEGIN
        writeln ('Roots are real:');
        rootofdisc := sqrt (disc);
        x1 := (-b + rootofdisc) / (2*a);
        x2 := (-b - rootofdisc) / (2*a);
        writeln (x1 :6:2, ' and ', x2 :6:2)
    END ELSE

    BEGIN
        writeln ('Roots are complex:');
        realpart := -b / (2*a);
        imagpart := sqrt(-disc) / (2*a);
        writeln (realpart :6:2, ' + ', imagpart :6:2, 'i  and  ',
                 realpart :6:2, ' - ', imagpart :6:2, 'i')
    END
END.
```

Figure 4.7

---

real and imaginary parts and include the letter "i" in the output. The
program of figure 4.7 does this.

4.4 Nested conditionals

A case limb or the statement following THEN or ELSE may itself be
conditional or contain a conditional statement. For example, the digit
naming program of figure 4.3 is improved if we test that the value of
"digit" is less than 10 before the case-statement is entered. The case-
statement is nested within an if-statement:

```
    IF digit <= 9 THEN
    CASE digit OF
        . . .
    END (* CASE *) ELSE
        writeln ('greater than 9')
```

Better still, we should also check for negative values:

```
IF digit < 0 THEN writeln ('negative') ELSE
   IF digit <= 9 THEN
   CASE digit OF
      . . .
   END (* CASE *) ELSE
      writeln ('greater than 9')
```

This is a particular example of the general form

```
IF ... THEN ... ELSE
   IF ... THEN ... ELSE
      . . .
         IF ... THEN ... ELSE ...
```

This results in successive tests being made until one holds, whereupon the statement following the appropriate THEN is obeyed. If none of the tests holds, the statement following the final ELSE is obeyed. If the final if-statement has no else-part and none of the tests holds, no statement is obeyed.

```
PROGRAM ChronologicalDates (input, output);

    (* Checks whether two dates are
       supplied in chronological order *)

   VAR
       d1, d2, m1, m2, y1, y2 : integer;

BEGIN
    writeln ('Type two dates, one per line,');
    writeln ('each in the form   day   month   year');
    readln (d1, m1, y1);   readln (d2, m2, y2);

    IF y1 < y2 THEN writeln ('In order') ELSE
     IF y1 > y2 THEN writeln ('Not in order') ELSE

       (* y1 = y2 *)
       IF m1 < m2 THEN writeln ('In order') ELSE
        IF m1 > m2 THEN writeln ('Not in order') ELSE

          (* y1 = y2, m1 = m2 *)
          IF d1 < d2 THEN writeln ('In order') ELSE
           IF d1 > d2 THEN writeln ('Not in order') ELSE

             (* y1 = y2, m1 = m2, d1 = d2 *)
             writeln ('The dates are the same')
END.
```

Figure 4.8

This structure is illustrated further by the program of figure 4.8 which determines whether two dates are supplied in chronological order. Each date is typed on a separate line as three integers:

> day month year

Initially only the years need be compared. If they differ, they determine the chronological ordering of the dates; only if the years are the same need the months be examined. By a similar argument, the days need be compared only if the two months then agree.

Using this same form we can extend our quadratic equation solver of figure 4.7 to recognise equal roots. The roots are equal when the discriminant is zero so our program wants the following structure.

```
IF disc > 0 THEN { distinct real roots } ELSE
  IF disc = 0 THEN { equal real roots } ELSE
    { complex roots }
```

This works perfectly well and you might like to try it. However, I want to extend the program to cater for equations with real coefficients and the outline above is no longer suitable. Because "disc" will now be a real variable, this outline does something we should never do. The operator = (and, similarly, <>) should not be applied to real operands. As our earlier discussion on the precision of reals showed, two expressions which are mathmatically equivalent can produce different values when evaluated by the computer. Consequently, if we wish to test equality of reals, we compare the magnitude of their difference with some suitably small number. So, if our quadratic equation program is to cater for real coefficients, it should include

```
CONST
  assumedzero = 1E-9;
```

and then the test

```
IF disc > 0 THEN
```

becomes

```
IF disc > assumedzero THEN
```

and the test

```
IF disc = 0 THEN
```

becomes

```
IF abs(disc) <= assumedzero THEN
```

Alternatively, the program could be written as in figure 4.9.

A short while ago we modified the program of figure 4.3 to check for integers outside the range [0,9]. We could have achieved this with the following program fragment

```
          IF digit >= 0 THEN
             IF digit <= 9 THEN
             CASE digit OF
                  . . .
             END (* CASE *) ELSE
                 writeln ('greater than 9')
          ELSE
             writeln ('negative')
```

```
    PROGRAM QuadEqn (input, output);

        (* Solves a quadratic equation *)

        CONST
           assumedzero = 1E-9;

        VAR
           a, b, c, x1, x2, disc, rootofdisc, repart, impart : real;

    BEGIN
       writeln ('Give the coefficients');
       readln (a, b, c);

       disc := sqr(b) - 4*a*c;

       IF disc > assumedzero THEN
       BEGIN
          writeln ('Distinct real roots:');
          rootofdisc := sqrt (disc);
          x1 := (-b + rootofdisc) / (2*a);
          x2 := (-b - rootofdisc) / (2*a);
          writeln (x1:6:2, ' and ', x2:6:2)
       END ELSE

          IF disc < -assumedzero THEN
          BEGIN
             writeln ('Complex roots:');
             repart := -b / (2*a);
             impart := sqrt(-disc) / (2*a);
             writeln (repart:6:2, ' + ', impart:6:2, 'i    and    ',
                      repart:6:2, ' - ', impart:6:2, 'i')
          END ELSE

          BEGIN
             writeln ('Equal real roots:');
             writeln (-b/(2*a) :6:2)
          END
    END.
```

Figure 4.9

---

but the program produced by this approach is less easy to follow. When IF immediately follows THEN it can be difficult (for the human reader) to sort out which ELSE goes with which THEN. This is particularly so when one of the if-statements has no else-part. Consider the following schema.

```
IF t1 THEN
    IF t2 THEN s1
ELSE s2
```

Pascal decrees that an ELSE is associated with its closest preceding outstanding THEN so your compiler will be in no doubt that, in this case, the ELSE will be associated with the second THEN. However, this may not be immediately apparent to the human reader. This is called the 'trailing ELSE problem'.

There are three ways to improve transparency in this context. One, often the best, is to rewrite this section of program so that the problem does not arise. Another is to replace one of the if-statements by a case-statement with a boolean selector and this will be described in chapter 8. The third is to use statement brackets to explicitly associate the ELSE with its intended THEN. BEGIN and END may be used to enclose a single statement. The earlier schema can be transformed into either

```
IF t1 THEN
BEGIN
    IF t2 THEN s1
END ELSE
    s2
```

to associate the ELSE with the first THEN or

```
IF t1 THEN
BEGIN
    IF t2 THEN s1 ELSE s2
END
```

to associate the ELSE with the second THEN.

4.5 Exercises

*1. Modify the electricity units program of exercise 2.7.3 to cater for the situation where the meter has reached 9999 and then returned to zero, thereby causing the previous reading to exceed the current reading.

*2. Write a program to determine whether a given triangle is right-angled assuming that the length of each side is specified as an integral number of units and the length of the hypotenuse is the last value supplied.

3. Modify the "BankBalance" program of figure 4.1 so that, for any negative balance printed, the minus sign precedes the dollar sign.

*4. Write a program which reads a month (an integer in the range 1 to 12) and, ignoring leap years, states the number of days in the month.

5. Write a program to print the Morse Code of any supplied digit.

```
0 -----    4 ....-    7 --...
1 .----    5 .....    8 ---..
2 ..---    6 -....    9 ----.
3 ...--
```

6. Modify the "Quadrants" program of figure 4.4 to cater for negative angles.

7. Extend your program for exercise 2 to include data validation. Your program is to check that the supplied lengths do specify a triangle.

8. Modify your program for exercise 3.3.13 to check that the supplied equation does have only one real root. If t>0 all three roots are real.

*9. Write a program which, given the ages in years of Jack and Jill, states who is the elder and by how many years. If Jack and Jill are the same age, the program should say so.

*10. Write a program to determine which is the largest of three given integers. {Hint: assign to a variable "max" the larger of the first two integers and then compare the value of "max" with the third integer.}

*11. Write a program to tell a person's age in years (not years, months and days). The person's birthdate and the current date are given, each in the form of three integers – day, month, year.

12. Extend your program for exercise 4 to read a year as well as a month and to cater for leap years. A century is not a leap year unless it is divisible by 400; otherwise a year is a leap year if it is divisible by 4. {Hint: test first for division by 400, then by 100 and, finally, by 4.}

*13. Write a program to accept a date typed in the form

    day month year

with the year specified by two digits, and to expand it by naming the month, quoting the full four digits of the year and following the day by st, nd, rd or th as appropriate. For example

    23 5 82

should appear as

    23rd MAY 1982

*14. Write a program to print three supplied integers in ascending order. {Hint: compare the first two and interchange their values if they are not in ascending order; then decide where the third value falls in relation to these two.}

CHAPTER 5
Character by Character

We have met the two scalar types "integer" and "real". A third scalar type is "char". It comprises all the characters available. As with the two arithmetic types we can define constants and variables of this type and we can read and write values of this type. A character constant is effectively a string of length 1. Here are some character constant definitions:

```
CONST
    space = ' ';
      dot = '.';
     zero = '0';
```

Notice that a space is a valid character. The end-of-line marker is also a valid character; in fact, it is really just a space character but, in chapter 8, we shall learn how to distinguish it from other spaces.

A variable of type "char" can take as its value any character in the set available. When a value is read into a character variable only one character is read from the input stream. This contrasts with the reading of arithmetic values when any leading spaces and ends of lines are ignored and a terminator must be supplied. Of course, if a character is read by "readln" it must be followed by (at least) an end-of-line character.

If the implementation is buffer driven then, whenever we wish the computer to respond immediately to a series of characters, we must follow the series by an end-of-line character. Consequently, we shall usually read such a series with "readln" rather than "read". Remember, though, the warning issued at the end of chapter 2; some systems behave very unsociably where character reading is concerned.

When a character is output then, unless a field width greater than 1 is specified, no extra spaces will be printed; the character will occupy only one character position. The program of figure 5.1 reads a four letter word and prints it backwards. No spaces will appear within the output word.

The characters available on a computer form an ordered sequence − this is called the lexicographic order. Associated with each character is an ordinal number, its position in the lexicographic order. The first character has ordinal number 0, the second ordinal number 1, and so on. Any data type whose values form a countable, ordered sequence is called an ordinal type. That is why "integer" was described as an ordinal type in chapter 2 (but "real" was not).

When the case-statement was introduced in section 4.2, the selector was described as an 'ordinal expression'. Characters can therefore be used as case-statement selectors. The program of figure 5.2 illustrates this and produces one of the names Amanda, Brian, Christine and Frank if given the initial. The case labels are not quoted in alphabetic order purposely to illustrate that their order is irrelevant.

```
PROGRAM Reverse4LetterWord (input, output);

    (* Reverses any four letter word *)

  VAR
     c1, c2, c3, c4 : char;

BEGIN
  write ('Please type a four-letter word ');
  readln (c1, c2, c3, c4);
  writeln ('Reversed, this is ', c4, c3, c2, c1)
END.
```

                         Figure 5.1

The relational operators, introduced in section 4.1, can be applied
to any two operands of (the same) ordinal type. When applied to
characters, they compare the positions of the two characters in the
lexicographic order. Unfortunately, the characters available and their
ordering vary from one computer to another. In all computer character
sets the upper case letters A, B, ..., Z and the digits 0, 1, ..., 9
appear in the order you would expect but some will place the digits
before the letters while others may have them the other way round.

```
PROGRAM  GiveName (input, output);

    (* Prints one of four names,
       given the initial *)

  VAR
     initial : char;

BEGIN
  write ('What is your initial? ');
  readln (initial);

  write ('Hello ');

  CASE initial OF
    'B' : writeln ('Brian');
    'A' : writeln ('Amanda');
    'F' : writeln ('Frank');
    'C' : writeln ('Christine')
  END (* CASE *)
END.
```

                         Figure 5.2

Consequently, we can assume that relations such as

```
'A' < 'Z'
'D' > 'C'
'7' >= '4'
```

will be true on all computers but relations such as

```
'9' < 'A'
'+' > '*'
'>' > '<'
```

may be true on some but false on others. You should avoid relying upon features which vary from one machine to another but, where such features must be introduced, mark them clearly with comments so that, if ever the program is moved to another machine, implementation dependent areas can be easily located.

Be clear in your mind of the difference between the characters '0', '1', ..., '9' and the integers 0, 1, ..., 9. We can assign characters to character variables, but we can't assign integers to character variables. On the other hand, we can multiply two integers, but we can't multiply two characters.

Lower case letters are not always available but, if they are, their ordering will be as you would expect. We shall assume that they are available and, when we need to know their position relative to the upper case letters, we shall assume that

```
'a' > 'Z'
```

The program of figure 5.3 prints two supplied three-letter words in alphabetical order. The process is similar to that of figure 4.8.

5.1 Standard functions

Within the lexicographic order, each character but the first has a predecessor and each but the last has a successor. Predecessors and successors are delivered by two functions.

```
pred  -  predecessor
succ  -  successor
```

Although it is not always the case, we shall assume that each of the three sets of characters

```
0, 1, ..., 9
A, B, ..., Z
a, b, ..., z
```

forms a contiguous sequence and, as mentioned earlier, that the upper case letters come somewhere before the lower case letters.

```
PROGRAM ThreeLetterWordsInOrder (input, output);

    (* Prints two three-letter words
       a and b in alphabetic order *)

   VAR
      a1, a2, a3, b1, b2, b3 : char;

BEGIN
   writeln ('Type two three-letter words, one per line');
   readln (a1, a2, a3);    readln (b1, b2, b3);

   IF a1 < b1 THEN writeln (a1,a2,a3, ' ', b1,b2,b3) ELSE
   IF a1 > b1 THEN writeln (b1,b2,b3, ' ', a1,a2,a3) ELSE

     IF a2 < b2 THEN writeln (a1,a2,a3, ' ', b1,b2,b3) ELSE
     IF a2 > b2 THEN writeln (b1,b2,b3, ' ', a1,a2,a3) ELSE

       IF a3 <= b3 THEN writeln (a1,a2,a3, ' ', b1,b2,b3) ELSE
          writeln (b1,b2,b3, ' ', a1,a2,a3)
END.
```

Figure 5.3

The program of figure 5.4 reads a letter, assumed to be in the range C to X (or c to x) and prints five consecutive letters centred on the supplied letter. Given the letter H the program will produce the output

        Five letters centred on H are FGHIJ

Two functions map between characters and their ordinal numbers.

        chr - delivers a character given its ordinal number

        ord - delivers the ordinal number of a supplied character

Subject to our assumption that letters are contiguous, the position in the alphabet of a lower case letter represented by a variable "l" is given by

        $ord(l) - ord('a') + 1$

and the letter at position "n" in the alphabet (if "n" is an integer variable with a value in the range 1 to 26) is given by

        $chr (ord('a') + n - 1)$

The functions "ord", "succ" and "pred" can be applied to items of any ordinal type.

```
---------------------------------------------------------------------------

      PROGRAM FiveLetters (input, output);

            (* Prints five consecutive letters centred on a
               supplied letter - assuming that the letters
               are contiguous in the computer character set *)

         VAR
            letter : char;

      BEGIN
         write ('Give me a letter ');    readln (letter);

         writeln ('Five letters centred on ', letter, ' are ',
                   pred(pred(letter)), pred(letter), letter,
                   succ(letter), succ(succ(letter)) )
      END.

                     Figure 5.4

---------------------------------------------------------------------------
```

5.2 Text files

We have talked informally of the input 'stream' and the output 'stream' implying a stream of characters flowing in to or out from a program. The formal term for a stream is <u>file</u> and, in particular, a file composed of characters and end-of-line markers is called a <u>text</u> file. You are probably already familiar with files. Your programs are probably stored in files. A program file contains lines of characters and so is itself a text file. Data files can be constructed in exactly the same way.

The two identifiers "input" and "output", used in the program heading, are the names of the <u>standard</u> text files, one to be used for reading and one for writing. Implementations vary but we shall assume that these always correspond to the terminal.

In chapter 13 we shall examine the whole aspect of files in detail; for the moment we see how a Pascal program can use external, non-standard, text files not associated with the terminal. There are four aspects to this.

1. All external files with which the program is to communicate must be named in the program heading.

2. Non-standard text files must be declared within the program as variables of type "text".

3. Before a non-standard file can be used it must be initialized either for reading or for writing. A file "f" is initialised for reading by the procedure call

        reset (f)

The procedure "reset" can be applied to the file several times during

the execution of a program and, each time, the file concerned is
initialised for reading from the beginning. Consequently, data stored in
a file can be scanned several times during one run of a program. We
shall see an illustration of this in chapter 6.

A file "g" is initialised for writing by the procedure call

        rewrite (g)

The file "f" must already exist (because it cannot otherwise be read).
The file "g" need not exist before the program is run. If it does exist,
it will be overwritten; if it does not, an empty file "g" will
automatically be created when the program is about to be run.

    4. To read from or write to a non-standard file the file name must
be supplied as the first parameter to the input/output procedure. For
example, two characters would be read from a text file "f" by a
statement of the form

        read (f, c1, c2)
  or readln (f, c1, c2)

and two characters would be written to a text file "g" by a statement of
the form

        write (g, c1, c2)
  or writeln (g, c1, c2)

    As an example we modify the program of figure 5.1 so that it reads
the four-letter word from a file, say "word", and produces the reversed
copy in another file, say "revword". The program is in figure 5.5.
Because the data is not coming from the terminal, no prompt is issued
before the readln-statement. To view the output, you would have to print
the output file, "revword", using the same facilities your computer
supplies for printing program files.

```
PROGRAM Reverse4 (word, revword);

    (* Reads a four-letter word from "word" and
       produces a reversed copy of this word in "revword" *)

  VAR
    word, revword : text;
    c1, c2, c3, c4 : char;

BEGIN
  reset (word);   rewrite (revword);
  readln (word, c1, c2, c3, c4);
  writeln (revword, 'Reversed word: ', c4, c3, c2, c1)
END.
```

                    Figure 5.5

Your implementation may enable you to associate files other than those named. For example, to run this program you might have to type a command like

        RUN Reverse4

but you may be able to supply a command something like

        RUN Reverse4 (infile, outfile)

and the program will use the actual file "infile" when the program refers to "word" and "outfile" in place of "revword". However, this is implementation dependent and is not part of Pascal. We shall assume that a program communicates only with the files named.

In the above example two non-standard files replaced the two standard files. There is no reason why one, or both, of the standard files should not remain. The names of the standard files can be supplied as parameters to reading and writing procedures and this is good practice when other files are also in use.

```
PROGRAM CopyAcross (input, a, b, c, output, d);

        (* Copies three integers to one file
           from any of three other files *)

    VAR
        a, b, c, d : text;
        i1, i2, i3 : integer;
        source : char;

BEGIN
    write (output, 'State source file (a, b or c): ');
    readln (input, source);

    CASE source OF
        'A', 'a' : BEGIN
                        reset (a);    readln (a, i1, i2, i3)
                   END;
        'B', 'b' : BEGIN
                        reset (b);    readln (b, i1, i2, i3)
                   END;
        'C', 'c' : BEGIN
                        reset (c);    readln (c, i1, i2, i3)
                   END
    END (* CASE *);

    rewrite (d);    writeln (d, i1, i2, i3);
    writeln (output, 'Data safely written to "d"')
END.
```

                        Figure 5.6

The program of figure 5.6 copies three integers from one file to another. The user must choose one of three possible source files.

The ordering of file names within the program heading is of no significance but you would be well advised to adopt some convention such as placing input files before output files as in this example.

If output has been generated in a file it is possible to print this file at any output device at a later date. If the device provides paginated output it might be useful to include end-of-page markers within the output file. The Pascal statement

          page (f)

will insert an end-of-page marker in the output file. When the file is printed at a suitable device this marker will cause a jump to the top of the next page. If the file is printed at a terminal, the effect of the page marker varies from one implementation to another. It might be ignored, it might produce one or two blank lines or it might clear the screen.

5.2.1 File buffers

It is sometimes desirable to examine the next character of a text file without actually reading it in. This facility is provided by the file buffer. Associated with any file "f" is a file buffer variable "f^". If "f" is a text file, "f^" is a character variable and its value is always a copy of the next character in the file. It should not be assigned to in the normal way; it acquires a new value when reading from "f" occurs or when it is explicitly updated by the procedure call

          get (f)

This merely 'throws away' the next character in the file "f" and "f^" will then acquire a copy of the one after.

We can now see that reading from a text file is actually achieved using "get". If "ch" is a character variable, then

          read (f, ch)

is equivalent to

          BEGIN
             ch := f^;   get (f)
          END

When a number is read from a text file the program reads the characters of the number one by one, constructing the internal numeric value in the process, until the file buffer contains a character which cannot possibly be part of the number.

A file buffer is associated with the standard file "input" and "input^" is usually referred to as the input window. The program of figure 5.7 uses the input window to decide whether to read an integer or a character. The program reads the price of a single item and calculates the cost of a pair, given that a 15% discount applies when two are bought. If the initial price is less than $1 it will be supplied as an integer followed by the letter 'c'; if not, it will be supplied as a real value preceded by the character '$'. The program must not attempt to read a number if the next character of the input stream is '$'. Also, we do not want it to skip a character if this is the first character of an integer. So, it examines the input window before reading anything.

```
PROGRAM PairPrice (input, output);

        (* Computes the discounted price of a pair,
           given the price of an individual item *)

    CONST
       discpercent = 15;

    VAR
       dollars, discfactor : real;
       cents : integer;

BEGIN
    discfactor := (100 - discpercent) / 100;
    write ('Give me a price: ');
    CASE input^ OF
       '$' :
          BEGIN
             get (input);    readln (dollars);
             dollars := dollars * 2 * discfactor;
             writeln ('Price of a pair is $', dollars :4:2)
          END;
       '1', '2', '3', '4', '5', '6', '7', '8', '9' :
          BEGIN
             readln (cents);
             cents := round (cents * 2 * discfactor);
             write ('Price of a pair is ');
             IF cents < 100 THEN writeln (cents :1, 'c') ELSE
                writeln ('$', cents/100 :4:2)
          END
    END (* CASE *)
END.
```

Figure 5.7

The unsociable behaviour mentioned earlier arises because some implementations insist that the value of "input^" always be defined. This means that, whenever your program reads a character, the system will insist that the character after it is typed; not because it wants to read it yet but just because it wants to give "input^" its next value. A sensible implementation will not give "input^" a new value until absolutely necessary. If you are lumbered with a 'greedy' implementation you should pester your supplier to rectify the situation and, in the meantime, do all character reading with "get" and "input^".

You can then determine for yourself when "input^" is to be given a new value.

For completeness, it should be noted that a file buffer is also associated with a file used for output. The current content of the file buffer "f^" is written to the file "f" by the procedure call

        put (f)

If "ch" is a character variable (or constant or function), then

        write (f, ch)

is equivalent to

        BEGIN
          f^ := ch;   put (f)
        END

Use of an output file buffer will be illustrated in chapter 13.

5.3 Exercises

*1. Find out how many characters are available on your computer and write a program to print the first, the last and the middle two of the lexicographic ordering. Denote the number of characters by a user-defined constant.

*2. Write a program to print a letter, given some other letter and the distance the two are apart in the alphabet.

 3. Write a program to decode and print a three-letter word supplied in coded form with each letter replaced by an integer in the range 1 to 26 indicating its position in the alphabet.

*4. Write a program which states how far apart in the alphabet two given letters are.

*5. Write a program to state whether three supplied letters are in alphabetical order.

*6. Write a program to read two digits and print their sum but with the constraint that the only variables you are allowed to read are character variables. This gives you an insight into the process the read-statement must perform when it is reading numbers.

 7. Write a program to print the Morse code of any letter.
```
        A .-     F ..-.   K -.-    O ---    S ...    W .--
        B -...   G --.    L .-..   P .--.   T -      X -..-
        C -.-.   H ....   M --     Q --.-   U ..-    Y -.--
        D -..    I ..     N -.     R .-.    V ...-   Z --..
        E .      J .---
```

*8. Write a program to act as a simple pocket calculator and evaluate
    an expression involving two numbers and one operator. Assume that
    there will be no spaces within the expression and constrain the
    operations available to addition, subtraction, multiplication and
    division. For example, given the data

        17.3+5.8

    your program should produce 23.1 as its output.

 9. A program is to read a letter followed by a three-letter word and
    is to state whether the specified letter is contained within the
    word. The letter and the word may be immediately adjacent or may be
    separated by either one or two spaces.

10. The set of characters available on your computer will include
    'control characters' for such purposes as moving the cursor on the
    screen. If you can determine the ordinal numbers of these
    characters, write a program to make the cursor traverse a square on
    the screen.

*11. Modify some of your programs to take their input from a file and
     some to produce output in a file.

CHAPTER 6
Round and Round

We often want computers to repeat some process several times. For example, computers are commonly used to work out company payrolls. For each employee, the computer is given appropriate details (hours worked, rate of pay and so on) and it works out that person's take-home pay. It does this for every employee; so it performs the same task over and over again, using different data each time.

When a program obeys a group of statements several times, it is said to be looping and loops are of two types. If we know how many times we wish to repeat the loop the situation is said to be deterministic; if not, it is non-deterministic.

For example, a mathematician might want to compute a particular term in a series (say, the fifteenth term). This would be a deterministic situation; he would write a section of program to compute the next term in the series and he would know how many times he wanted that section obeyed. On the other hand, he may want the first term which satisfies some condition but not know which term that will be. Now the situation is non-deterministic; he must keep generating terms until the condition is satisfied.

Non-deterministic loops are the subject of chapter 7. In this chapter we concentrate on deterministic loops.

A deterministic loop is implemented by a for-statement. It is controlled by a control variable which, in some sense, counts the repetitions and it can be incremented (and so count up) or decremented (and so count down). The control variable will be updated automatically; you must make no attempt to change the value of the control variable within the loop. Upon exit from the loop, the value of the control variable will be undefined.

Chapter 9 will introduce the notion of "scope" of a variable. It will be pointed out then that a control variable must be declared within the most local scope. Read this paragraph again when you have read Chapter 9.

The general form of an incremental for-statement is

> FOR v := e_1 TO e_2 DO s
>
> where v is a variable of some ordinal type, say t,
> e_1 and e_2 are expressions of type t
> and   s is any statement.

If $e_1 > e_2$ the loop body (s) is not obeyed at all; otherwise the body is executed

$$\text{ord}(e_2) - \text{ord}(e_1) + 1$$

times. Each execution of the loop body is called an <u>iteration</u>. For successive iterations the control variable, v, takes successive values

$$e_1, \text{succ}(e_1), \text{succ}(\text{succ}(e_1)), \ldots, e_2.$$

    The program of figure 6.1 uses this form to generate a file containing a list of characters, together with their ordinal numbers. Note that some characters are <u>control</u> characters reserved for special purposes and printing them at a terminal may have no effect.

```
PROGRAM CharSet (chars);

    (* Generates the computer character set *)

CONST
   noofchars = 128;

VAR
   chars : text;
   i : integer;

BEGIN
   rewrite (chars);
   writeln (chars, 'ord chr');
   FOR i := 0 TO noofchars-1 DO
      writeln (chars, i :3, chr(i) :4)
END.
```

                            Figure 6.1

    The general form of a decremental for-statement is

```
            FOR v := e1 DOWNTO e2 DO s

     where   v is a variable of some ordinal type, say t,
             e1 and e2 are expressions of type t
     and     s is any statement.
```

    If $e_1 < e_2$ the loop body (s) is not obeyed at all; otherwise the loop body is obeyed

$$\text{ord}(e_1) - \text{ord}(e_2) + 1$$

times. For each successive iteration of the loop body the control variable, v, takes successive values

$$e_1, \text{pred}(e_1), \text{pred}(\text{pred}(e_1)), \ldots, e_2.$$

    In most deterministic loop situations the obvious order of sequencing for the control variable is up; but sometimes it is more

---

```
PROGRAM TenGreenBottles (output);

    (* Prints the words of "Ten Green Bottles" *)

VAR
    n : integer;

BEGIN
    FOR n := 10 DOWNTO 1 DO
    BEGIN
        writeln (n:2, ' green bottles hanging on the wall');
        writeln (n:2, ' green bottles hanging on the wall');
        writeln ('But if one green bottle',
                 ' should accidentally fall');
        writeln ('There''d be ', n-1:1,
                 ' green bottles hanging on the wall');
        writeln
    END
END.
```

Figure 6.2

---

natural to work down. This happens quite often in children's songs. The program of figure 6.2 prints the words of all ten verses of a well known song. Notice that, because the loop body is to contain more than one statement, these statements must be bracketed between BEGIN and END.

The program of figure 6.3 utilises a character control variable and uses both an incremental and a decremental for-statement to print the alphabet forwards and backwards.

```
PROGRAM Alphabets (output);

    (* Prints the alphabet forwards and backwards *)

VAR
    l : char;

BEGIN
    FOR l := 'a' TO 'z' DO write (l);
    writeln;

    FOR l := 'z' DOWNTO 'a' DO write (l);
    writeln
END.
```

Figure 6.3

```
PROGRAM RaiseToKnownPower (input, output);

(* Raises a number x to a non-negative integer power n *)

   VAR
      x, y : real;
      n, power : integer;

BEGIN
   write ('Please give me a number ');   readln (x);
   write ('To what power would you like it raised? ');
   readln (n);

   y := 1;
   FOR power := 1 TO n DO
      y := y * x;

   writeln (x, ' raised to the power ', n :1, ' is ', y :9:4)
END.
```

Figure 6.4

```
PROGRAM RaiseToKnownPower (input, output);

(* Raises a number x to a non-negative integer power n *)

   VAR
      x, xsquared, y : real;
      n, power : integer;

BEGIN
   write ('Please give me a number ');   readln (x);
   write ('To what power would you like it raised? ');
   readln (n);

   IF n = 0 THEN y := 1 ELSE
   BEGIN
      xsquared := sqr (x);
      IF n MOD 2 = 0 THEN y := 1 ELSE y:= x;
      FOR power := 1 TO n DIV 2 DO
         y := y * xsquared
   END;

   writeln (x, ' raised to the power ', n :1, ' is ', y :9:4)
END.
```

Figure 6.5

A loop body need not refer to the control variable. The program of figure 6.4 raises a number to a specified power and the control variable merely governs the number of iterations. For this program, we can reduce the number of iterations if we observe that

$$\text{if } n \text{ is even } (n = 2k, \text{ say}) \text{ then } x^n = (x^2)^k \text{ and}$$

$$\text{if } n \text{ is odd } (n = 2k+1, \text{ say}) \text{ then } x^n = x(x^2)^k.$$

We can detect an even n with the test

$$n \text{ MOD } 2 = 0$$

The program of figure 6.5 computes the same value as that of figure 6.4 but uses the square of x rather than x.

```
PROGRAM LoanRepay (input, output);

    (* Computes final balance and total interest for
       a loan reduced by equal monthly instalments *)

  CONST
    noofyears = 10;       intpercent = 15;

  VAR
    year : integer;
    monthpay, yearpay, sum, interest,
      totinterest, intrate : real;

BEGIN
  write ('How much do you wish to borrow? $');
  readln (sum);
  write ('How much do you intend to repay each month? $');
  readln (monthpay);

  intrate := intpercent / 100;
  yearpay := 12 * monthpay;

  totinterest := 0;
  FOR year := 1 TO noofyears DO
  BEGIN
    interest := sum * intrate;
    totinterest := totinterest + interest;
    sum := sum + interest - yearpay
  END;

  writeln ('After ', noofyears :1, ' years');
  writeln ('  the outstanding balance is $', sum :4:2);
  writeln ('  and the total interest paid is $', totinterest :4:2)
END.
```

Figure 6.6

The program of figure 6.2 showed that a loop body may comprise several statements if they are bracketed to form a compound statement. This is further illustrated by the program of figure 6.6. This program computes the amount of a loan outstanding and the total interest paid after equal monthly repayments have been made over a ten year period. Interest, at the rate of 15%, is added to the current balance at the start of each year.

Notice that an effort has been made to avoid unnecessary calculation within the loop. The quantities "intpercent/100" and "12*monthpay" are needed inside the loop but their values do not change during execution of the loop. Consequently, they are each evaluated once, before the loop is entered, rather than during every iteration of the loop body.

We conclude this section with a more realistic example. A file, "markfile", contains the marks obtained by a number of students in a Pascal Programming examination. These marks are in the range 0 to 100 and are supplied one per line. Each mark is followed by the name of a candidate, supplied as a sequence of 20 characters. The very first entry in the file is an integer indicating the number of students. So, for a small group, the data might be as follows.

```
5
13              A. Fool
97            B. A. Head
6              B. Hind
73           I. Swotalot
2          Ivor Thickhead
```

We wish to know the highest mark achieved and the overall average. We also require the names of those students with the highest mark and of those who have failed. To pass the examination, a student must obtain a mark which is at least 2/3 of the average. Thus, if the average were 60, the pass mark would be 40.

We shall have to scan the data more than once. Before we can read through the file printing the names of students with marks less than 2/3 of the average, we must compute the average and this entails reading all the marks. We shall therefore have to make use of a facility mentioned in section 5.2 and initialize the file for reading more than once.

Let us consider the activities which will require a complete scan of the data.
1. Compute the average - sum the marks and divide by the number of students.
2. List the failures - scan the file and print the name of each student with a mark below the pass mark.
3. Determine the top mark - scan the file and keep a record of the highest mark encountered.
4. List the holders of the top mark - scan the file and print the name of each student with the top mark.

We could arrange for our program to read the file four times and perform the actions in the order described but this would be rather wasteful if some activities could be conducted in parallel. Activities 1 and 3 can

easily be carried out together. While reading the marks we can form a
running total and keep a record of the highest encountered. Activities 2
and 3 could be carried out together but we would then get the two lists
of names interleaved. If both lists are to be output to the same file it
is better to perform separate scans so that one list will completely
follow the other. An alternative solution is to produce the two lists in
separate files; there is then no objection to producing both lists
during one scan of the data. Our overall program structure is then

            Compute top mark and average;
            List top mark holders and failures

We compute the average mark with a program fragment of the form shown in
figure 6.7.

```
VAR
    markfile : text;
    noofstudents, total, mark, stud : integer;
    average : real;

   . . .

reset (markfile);
read (markfile, noofstudents);
total := 0;
FOR stud := 1 TO noofstudents DO
BEGIN
    readln (markfile, mark);    total := total + mark
END;
average := total / noofstudents;
```

Figure 6.7

We read each mark with "readln" so that the student's name is ignored.
To record the highest mark encountered we introduce a variable

        topmark : integer;

initialized to 0 prior to entry to the loop. Within the loop, we compare
each mark read from the file with the current highest. If a mark exceeds
the current highest, we note this as the current highest:

        IF mark > topmark THEN
            topmark := mark

We now reinitialize the file and scan the data again, but this time
reading each mark with "read" rather than "readln". If a mark is either
the top mark or below the pass mark, we copy the next 20 characters to
the appropriate output file. The complete program is in figure 6.8. For
completeness it also counts the number of failures and the number of
students with the top mark.

```
PROGRAM ExamMarks (markfile, tops, fails);

   (* Given a file of examination marks and names, this program
      produces a file of top mark holders and a file of failures.
      The pass mark is taken to be 2/3 of the average mark. *)

   CONST
     namelength = 20;

   VAR
     markfile, tops, fails : text;
     noofstudents, topcount, failcount, total,
       mark, topmark, passmark, stud, chcount : integer;
     average : real;
     ch : char;

BEGIN
   (* Compute top mark and average *)
   reset (markfile);   readln (markfile, noofstudents);
   topmark := 0;   total := 0;
   FOR stud := 1 TO noofstudents DO
   BEGIN
     readln (markfile, mark);   total := total + mark;
     IF mark > topmark THEN
       topmark := mark
   END;
   average := total / noofstudents;

   (* List top mark holders and failures *)
   rewrite (tops);   rewrite (fails);
   writeln (tops, 'Number of candidates: ', noofstudents :1);
   writeln (fails, 'Number of candidates: ', noofstudents :1);

   writeln (tops, 'Average mark: ', average :4:1);
   writeln (fails, 'Average mark: ', average :4:1);

   writeln (tops, 'Highest mark: ', topmark :1);
   writeln (tops);
   writeln (tops, 'Candidates with highest mark:');

   passmark := trunc(2 * average / 3);
   writeln (fails, 'Pass mark: ', passmark :1);
   writeln (fails);
   writeln (fails, 'Candidates below pass mark:');

   reset (markfile);   readln (markfile, noofstudents);
   topcount := 0;   failcount := 0;
   FOR stud := 1 TO noofstudents DO
   BEGIN
     read (markfile, mark);
     IF mark < passmark THEN
     BEGIN
       failcount := failcount + 1;
```

```
              FOR chcount := 1 TO namelength DO
              BEGIN
                read (markfile, ch);    write (fails, ch)
              END;
              writeln (fails)
           END ELSE
              IF mark = topmark THEN
              BEGIN
                topcount := topcount + 1;
                FOR chcount := 1 TO namelength DO
                BEGIN
                  read (markfile, ch);    write (tops, ch)
                END;
                writeln (tops)
              END;
           readln (markfile)
        END;

        writeln (tops);
        writeln (tops, 'Number of candidates: ', topcount :1);
        writeln (fails);
        writeln (fails, 'Number of candidates: ', failcount :1)
     END.
```

Figure 6.8

Notice that, as each character of a name is being copied, it is held in
a character variable but this is not necessary; the following loop will
copy "n" characters from one text file "f" to another text file "g".

```
        FOR i := 1 TO n DO
        BEGIN
           write (g, f^);    get (f)
        END
```

6.1 Nested Loops

When one loop occurs within the body of another, the loops are said to
be nested and we illustrate this by returning to the program of figure
6.2. In the song "Ten Green Bottles", the first line is sung twice so,
rather than write the same Pascal statement twice, we can write it once
and put it inside a loop which will obey it twice. This is done in the
program of figure 6.9.

     In that example, both loops go up. Following our musical theme, we
can show how one loop might go up, while the other comes down. A program
to print the words of "The Twelve Days of Christmas" would follow the
outline shown in figure 6.10.

     To give a more practical application of nested loops, we shall now
write a program to draw a histogram. Let us assume that the examination
mark program of figure 6.8 has been extended to produce a file of

---

```
    PROGRAM TenGreenBottles (output);

        (* Prints the words of "Ten Green Bottles" *)

        VAR
          n, times : integer;
    BEGIN
      FOR n := 10 DOWNTO 1 DO
      BEGIN
        FOR times := 1 TO 2 DO
          writeln (n:2, ' green bottles hanging on the wall');
        writeln ('But if one green bottle',
                 ' should accidentally fall');
        writeln ('There''d be ', n-1:1,
                 ' green bottles hanging on the wall');
        writeln
      END
    END.
```
                        Figure 6.9

---

frequency counts of marks falling in each of the following intervals.

```
    0 -  9   10 - 19   20 - 29   30 - 39   40 - 49
   50 - 59   60 - 69   70 - 79   80 - 89   90 - 99
```

The program of figure 6.11 produces a file containing ten lines of stars, the number of stars in each line being dictated by the frequency counts. Each line of stars is preceded by the mid-point value of the interval to which it corresponds.

The loop which prints a line of stars is nested within the loop which reads the frequencies and so the two loops must use different control variables.

```
    FOR this := 1 TO 12 DO
    BEGIN
       writeln ('On the', this, ' day of Christmas');
       writeln ('My true love sent to me');

       State present received on this day of Christmas;

       FOR earlier := this-1 DOWNTO 1 DO
          State present received on earlier day of Christmas;
       writeln
    END
```
                        Figure 6.10

```
PROGRAM DrawHistogram (freqfile, histogram);

    (* Produces a histogram of frequency counts *)

  CONST
    noofintervals = 10;
    histchar = '*';        space = ' ';

  VAR
    freqfile, histogram : text;
    interval, frequency, chcount : integer;

BEGIN
  reset (freqfile);   rewrite (histogram);
  FOR interval := 1 TO noofintervals DO
  BEGIN
    read (freqfile, frequency);
    write (histogram, interval*10-5 :2, space);
    FOR chcount := 1 TO frequency DO
      write (histogram, histchar);
    writeln (histogram)
  END
END.
```

                        Figure 6.11

Notice that the inner loop caters even for a zero frequency count; if the frequency read is less than 1, the loop has no effect. When supplied with the data

        4 6 2 4 14 20 26 30 22 12

the program produces the following output.

```
 5 ****
15 ******
25 **
35 ****
45 **************
55 ********************
65 **************************
75 ******************************
85 **********************
95 ************
```

6.2 Exercises

*1. Modify your program for exercise 1.6.1 so that ten rockets follow one another travelling up the screen.

 2. Write a program to produce a table of the integers 1 to 20 together with their squares and reciprocals.

*3. Write a program to print an 'n times table' for a given integer n. For n=7, the output should be of the following form:

```
 1 * 7  =   7
 2 * 7  =  14
      . . .
12 * 7  =  84
```

*4. Write a program to print all the letters of the alphabet between two supplied letters (inclusive). The letters are to be printed in the order in which the specified letters are supplied. For example,

```
DH  =>  DEFGH

TM  =>  TSRQPONM
```

*5. 'n factorial', usually written n!, is defined to be the product of all the integers in the range 1 to n.

```
n! = 1 * 2 * 3 * ... * n
```

Write a program which computes n! for a given positive n.

 6. A text file contains an integer n followed by a set of n measurements x_1, x_2, ..., x_n. Write a program to compute the mean X and standard deviation S of this sample.

$$X = (\sum_{i=1}^{n} x_i)/n \qquad S^2 = (\sum_{i=1}^{n} x_i^2)/n - X^2$$

*7. A file contains an integer n followed by n numbers, some positive and some negative. Write a program to compute the average of the positive numbers and the average of the negative numbers.

 8. A file contains an integer n followed by n examination marks in the range 0 to 99. Write a program to produce a file of frequency counts of marks falling in each of the four intervals
0 - 19, 20 - 39, 40 - 59, 60 - 79, 80 - 99.

 9. Apart from the number 1, there are only four positive integers which are equal to the sum of the cubes of their digits. One of these is 153 because

$$1^3 + 5^3 + 3^3 = 1 + 125 + 27 = 153$$

Given that all four lie between 150 and 410, write a program to compute them.

*10. Write a program which reads a file of distinct integers and prints the two smallest and the two largest integers present. The first integer in the file is not part of the data set proper but indicates how many integers follow.

*11. Each verse of "Ten Green Bottles" contains 41 notes. In the key of C these are as given below. Write a program to determine the length of the longest ascending sequence of consecutive notes between C and G (eg CDE) and to state how many times a consecutive ascending sequence of this length occurs. Then modify your program to handle descending sequences instead.

   CCCEDCDECEEEGFEFGECCAAGECDEDCAGACCCEDCDEC

Store the notes in a file and arrange for your program to scan the file twice - first to determine the length of the longest sequence, and then to count the number of occurrences of sequences of this length.

12. Write a program which computes the total number of presents that, according to 'The twelve days of Christmas', my true love gave to me.

*13. Write a program which takes a positive value n and produces an inverted pyramid comprising n lines such that the value n appears n times in the first line of the pyramid, the value n-1 appears n-1 times in the second line, and so on. For n=5 the pyramid should have the following form.

```
5 5 5 5 5
 4 4 4 4
  3 3 3
   2 2
    1
```

14. Write a program which draws a diamond of the form illustrated below. The letter which is to appear at the widest point of the figure (E in the example) is specified as input data.

15. Write a program which prints the words of the children's song "One
    Man Went to Mow". The last verse is

        "10 men went to mow, went to mow a meadow;
        10 men, 9 men, 8 men, 7 men, 6 men,
         5 men, 4 men, 3 men, 2 men, 1 man and his dog
        Went to mow a meadow."

    In each previous verse the initial number of men is one less and in
    the first verse there is only one man and his dog.

16. If your Pascal system allows you to control cursor movement, write
    a program to produce a flight of steps diagonally across your
    terminal screen. Then write a program to draw a (square) spiral on
    the screen.

CHAPTER 7
. . . Until You're Finished

Pascal provides two non-deterministic loops: a while-statement and a repeat-statement.

7.1 While-statement

The general form is

```
        WHILE t DO s

    where  t is a test
    and    s is any statement.
```

The test (t) is made <u>prior</u> to each execution of the loop body (s). If the test proves false, control leaves the while-statement and passes to the statement next in sequence after the while-statement. If the test holds true, the loop body is obeyed and the process repeated until the test eventually proves false. If the test is false upon first entry, the loop body is not entered at all.

```
    The body of a while-loop need not be executed
```

So, here are some guidelines for using WHILE.

```
    A while-loop is appropriate when
        we don't know how many times
        we want the loop body obeyed
    and
        it may be not at all
```

The program of figure 7.1 performs a function similar to that of figure 5.1. It reverses a supplied four-letter word but skips any spaces or ends-of-lines which may precede the word. We are assuming that there may be no spaces before the word, in which case the loop will need to be obeyed zero times. So, we use a while-loop.

The program of figure 7.2 detects whether a given integer is prime or composite. A number is said to be prime if it has no factors other than 1 and itself. The program divides the supplied number n by successive integers 2, 3, ... until a factor is found (that is, until n MOD d = 0). If the first factor found is less than n then n is composite; if the first factor is n itself then n is prime. We don't know, in advance, how many divisors we shall have to try so the situation is non-deterministic. The first divisor tried (2) may be a factor and in this case we would not wish to execute the loop body;

```
    PROGRAM Reverse4 (input, output);

        (* Reverses a four-letter word
           optionally preceded by spaces *)

    CONST
      space = ' ';

    VAR
      c1, c2, c3, c4 : char;
BEGIN
    writeln ('Please type a four-letter word');

    WHILE input^ = space DO
      get (input);
    readln (c1, c2, c3, c4);

    writeln ('Reversed, this is ', c4, c3, c2, c1)
END.
```

Figure 7.1

```
    PROGRAM PrimeTester (input, output);

        (* Determines primality of an integer *)

    VAR
      d, n : integer;

BEGIN
    write ('Give me an integer ');    readln (n);

    IF n < 2 THEN
      writeln ('  *** too small ***') ELSE
    BEGIN
      d := 2;
      WHILE n MOD d <> 0 DO
        d := d + 1;

      IF d = n THEN
        writeln (n, ' is prime')
      ELSE
        writeln (n, ' is composite')
    END
END.
```

Figure 7.2

---

consequently we use a while-loop. The efficiency of this program can be improved and we shall return to this example later.

If we wish to include more than one statement within the body of a while-loop we must bracket them within BEGIN and END. The program of figure 7.3 is an extension of that of figure 7.1. It counts how many spaces precede the supplied word.

```
PROGRAM Reverse4 (input, output);

       (* Reverses a four-letter word
          optionally preceded by spaces *)

    CONST
       space = ' ';

    VAR
       c1, c2, c3, c4 : char;
       noofspaces : integer;

BEGIN
    writeln ('Please type a four-letter word');

    noofspaces := 0;
    WHILE input^ = space DO
    BEGIN
       noofspaces := noofspaces + 1;    get (input)
    END;

    readln (c1, c2, c3, c4);
    writeln ('Reversed, this is ', c4, c3, c2, c1);
    write ('The word was preceded by ',
                    noofspaces :1, 'space');
    IF noofspaces <> 1 THEN writeln ('s') ELSE
          writeln
END.
```

Figure 7.3

7.2 Repeat statement

The general form is

```
            REPEAT
                 s_1;  s_2;  ...;  s_n
            UNTIL t

      where  t is a test
      and    s_1, s_2, ..., s_n are any statements.
```

The test (t) is made <u>after</u> each execution of the loop body (s_1, s_2, ...,
s_n). If the test holds <u>true</u>, the loop is terminated and control passes
to the statement next in sequence after the repeat-statement. If the
test proves false, control returns to the start of the loop body and the
whole process is repeated until the test eventually holds true. Once the
loop is under way, a while-loop and a repeat-loop are equivalent. The
difference is upon first entry. With WHILE, the test is made <u>before</u> the
first execution of the loop body; with REPEAT, the test is made <u>after</u>
the first execution.

> The body of a repeat-loop is obeyed at least once

Here are guidelines for using REPEAT.

> A repeat-loop is appropriate when
>   we don't know how many times
>   we want the loop body obeyed
> but
>   it must be <u>at least once</u>.

The program of figure 7.4 determines the last letter of a supplied
word. The program assumes that no spaces or ends-of-lines will precede
the word but that the word is followed by at least one space or end-
of-line. The program reads characters until a space character follows. A
word must contain <u>at least one</u> letter and so <u>at least one</u> character must
be read. So, we use REPEAT.

```
PROGRAM LastLetter (input, output);

    (* Determines last letter of a supplied word *)

    CONST
      space = ' ';

    VAR
      letter : char;

BEGIN
    write ('What is your word? ');

    REPEAT
       read (letter)
    UNTIL input^ = space;

    writeln;
    writeln ('Its last letter is ', letter)
END.
```

                    Figure 7.4

```
    PROGRAM DoubleLetters (input, output);

        (* Counts the number of occurrences of
           double letters in a supplied word *)

    CONST
       space = ' ';

    VAR
       thisletter : char;
       doublecount : integer;
BEGIN
    write ('What is your word? ');

    doublecount := 0;
    REPEAT
       read (thisletter);
       IF input^ = thisletter THEN
          doublecount := doublecount + 1
    UNTIL input^ = space;

    writeln;
    writeln ('Number of double letters: ', doublecount :1)
END.
```

Figure 7.5

More than one statement can be included within the body of a repeat-loop without being bracketed between BEGIN and END. This is illustrated in figure 7.5. This program is similar to that of figure 7.4 but, rather than determine the last letter of the supplied word, it counts the number of 'double letters' within the word. For example, if supplied with the word

ACCOMMODATE

the program will report two double letters (CC and MM).

The program of figure 7.6 computes the smallest Fibonacci number greater than some specified bound. The first two terms of the Fibonacci sequence are 0 and 1. Each successive term is the sum of the previous two. The program insists that the bound be greater than 1 and we must therefore compute at least one new term. So we use REPEAT.

7.3 Data sentinels

A common requirement is to read an arbitrarily long sequence of values. Some arrangement must then be made to indicate the end of the sequence.

For example, when the loan repayment program of figure 6.6 is run, the user will probably want to compare several different repayments.

```
PROGRAM MinFib (input, output);

    (* Computes the smallest Fibonacci
       number which exceeds a specified bound *)

   VAR
       bound, thisterm, prevterm, termbeforethat : integer;
BEGIN
   write ('Specify the bound ');   readln (bound);

   IF bound < 1 THEN
      writeln ('  *** bound is too small ***') ELSE
   BEGIN
      thisterm := 1;   prevterm := 0;
      REPEAT
         termbeforethat := prevterm;   prevterm := thisterm;
         thisterm := prevterm + termbeforethat
      UNTIL thisterm > bound;

      writeln ('Smallest Fibonacci number greater than ',
               bound :1, ' is ', thisterm :1)
   END
END.
```

Figure 7.6

With the program in its present form, only one repayment can be
supplied. The program would be more useful if it accepted an arbitrary
number of different repayments. We would then need some way of knowing
when the user no longer wishes to suggest further repayments. One
approach is to ask the user, at the end of each iteration of the loop,
if he wishes to supply another figure and repeat the loop only if the
reply is "yes". Assuming the reply is either "yes" or "no" we need read
only the first letter. The modified program is in figure 7.7.

Sometimes we know of some values which cannot occur within the
supplied data and we can use one of these as a data sentinel. In the
example just considered, a repayment must be positive so we could
interpret any negative value as a data sentinel. Rather than ask if
another value is to be supplied, the program would insist that values
are supplied until a negative value is encountered. We illustrate the
use of a data sentinel with an example which reads from a file.

Consider the examination mark totalling process of figure 6.7, with
the modification that the data file contains no indication of the number
of marks present but the final line of the file contains a negative
integer. We must now write our program so that it reads the sentinel and
recognises it but does not process it.

```
PROGRAM LoanRepayments (input, output);

        (* Computes final balance and total interest
           for a loan reduced by equal monthly instalments.
           Several different repayments are accepted. *)

    CONST
        noofyears = 10;        intpercent = 15;

    VAR
        year : integer;
        monthpay, yearpay, sum, balance,
           interest, totinterest, intrate : real;
        reply : char;

BEGIN
    write ('How much do you wish to borrow? $');
    readln (sum);

    REPEAT
        write ('How much do you intend to repay each month? $');
        readln (monthpay);

        balance := sum;
        intrate := intpercent / 100;
        yearpay := 12 * monthpay;

        totinterest := 0;
        FOR year := 1 TO noofyears DO
        BEGIN
           interest := balance * intrate;
           totinterest := totinterest + interest;
           balance := balance + interest - yearpay
        END;

        writeln ('After ', noofyears :1, ' years');
        writeln ('  the outstanding balance is $', balance :4:2);
        writeln ('  and the total interest paid is $',
                                            totinterest :4:2);

        write ('Do you wish to supply another repayment? ');
        readln (reply)
    UNTIL reply = 'n';

    writeln ('OK - good bye')
END.
```

Figure 7.7

Our first attempt might be

```
reset (markfile);
total := 0;    noofstudents := 0;
REPEAT
   noofstudents := noofstudents + 1;
   readln (markfile, mark);    total := total + mark
UNTIL mark < 0
```

This is incorrect because, although the end of the sequence is recognised and the loop terminated, the data sentinel has been counted as a student's mark and added into the running total. We rectify this if we follow the loop by the two assignments

```
noofstudents := noofstudents - 1;
total := total - mark
```

but this is not the right approach. We should modify our program so that the data sentinel is neither counted as a mark nor added into the running total in the first place. This implies that the loop termination test must be made before the input value has been processed. This gives us

```
reset (markfile);
total := 0;    noofstudents := 0;
REPEAT
   noofstudents := noofstudents + 1;
   total := total + mark;    readln (markfile, mark)
UNTIL mark < 0
```

and now "mark" must be given a value before the loop is entered. We could give "mark" the value 0 prior to entry to the loop (and initialize "noofstudents" to -1). We would then get the right answer but the first two statements obeyed upon entry to the loop would be effectively

```
noofstudents := -1 + 1;    total := 0 + 0
```

and perhaps a better approach is possible. Ideally, we should initialize "mark" to the first input value. This is done in figure 7.8. This accumulates the correct total subject to the assumption that the sequence does contain at least one mark.

```
reset (markfile);
total := 0;    noofstudents := 0;
readln (markfile, mark);
REPEAT
   noofstudents := noofstudents + 1;
   total := total + mark;    readln (markfile, mark)
UNTIL mark < 0
```

Figure 7.8

7.4 Loop construction

A non-deterministic loop has three main constituents: initialization, body and termination. We now make some general observations about these in the order in which we construct them.

7.4.1 Loop body

When writing a loop body we assume it will be performed several times and write it in such a way that it will function correctly once it 'gets going'. We must convince ourselves that each iteration of the loop will perform the appropriate computation. Although at this stage we need not know the precise nature of the loop termination test, we must have some notion as to when we wish to exit from the loop so as to avoid superfluous (and possibly harmful) computation. So, when we have written a loop body we should know why we want control to leave the loop but perhaps we do not yet know how to detect the situation.

7.4.2 Loop termination

Once we know what is happening each time round a loop we can decide how to stop it. The termination condition must make use of some information which changes (or possibly changes) with each iteration, for otherwise the loop would become infinite! If the information you wish to incorporate within your test is not being changed by the loop body, then either you are thinking of the wrong test or your loop body is incomplete (or just plain wrong)! If you are sure your test is the right one then you must modify your loop body.

When you have ensured that the termination test involves information which can change within the loop you must convince yourself that it changes in such a way that the termination test will eventually be satisfied. Consider the loop

```
REPEAT
    IF n < m THEN
    BEGIN
        n := n + 2;    ...
    END ELSE
    BEGIN
        n := n - 2;    ...
    END
UNTIL n = m
```

for two integer variables "n" and "m". It might appear sensible at first sight; each iteration performs an assignment to "n" and each new value of "n" is apparently closer to the value of "m". A little thought shows that, unless "n" or "m" is referred to elsewhere within the loop, the process is finite only if "n" and "m" have the same parity. If one is odd and the other even the loop goes on forever!

When you have sorted out your loop body and termination test you should definitely know whether you want WHILE or REPEAT. If you want the termination test to be made before the first iteration use WHILE; if not, use REPEAT.

7.4.3 Loop initialization

We have written our loop body and termination test so that all will be
well so long as the loop starts off properly. Now we must ensure that
the 'computational state' is appropriate when the loop is first entered.

Variables used inside a loop often need initializing before the
loop is entered. This is particularly true for summing and counting
variables. Thus in figures 7.3, 7.5 and 7.8 the counting variables
"noofspaces", "doublecount" and "noofstudents" and the summing variable
"total" are initialized (to 0), in the prime testing program of figure
7.2 "d" is initialized (to 2), in the program "MinFib" of figure 7.6 the
two variables "thisterm" and "prevterm" are initialized (to 1 and 0
respectively) and in figure 7.7 the summing variable "totinterest" is
initialized (to 0).

Notice that each of these initializations is delayed. Each
initialization statement is usually as close to its loop as is
practicable. In the prime testing program, for example, "d" could be
initialized anywhere between the initial BEGIN of the program body and
the start of the loop which increments it but it is bad practice to do
it anywhere other than immediately before the loop. This variable has
nothing to do with any previous processing and so should not be mixed up
with it. Try to keep together statements which are logically connected.

7.5 Random numbers

Programs are often written to simulate events which occur in no
predictable sequence. Examples might be the arrival of customers at a
shop or the outcomes of successive tosses of a coin or throws of a die.
To do this, a program generates a sequence of 'random numbers' in some
particular range. To simulate throws of a six-sided die, these would be
integers in the range [1,6]; for the tossing of a coin they might be
integers in the range [0,1]. So that a program may be run several times
with the same sequence of numbers it is desirable that the numbers be
generated in some deterministic way. For this reason, they are called
'pseudo random numbers'.

One technique is to apply the following recurrence relation

$$x_{i+1} = (ax_i + b) \text{ MOD } c$$

for suitable values of a, b and c. The series of values $x_0, x_1, x_2, \ldots$ is
cyclic; that is, it repeats with a certain period. If a, b and c have
the following forms

$$c = 2^p$$
$$b = 2q + 1$$
$$a = 4b + 1$$

where p and q are any integers and x_0 lies in [0,c-1], then every
integer in the range [0,c-1] will be generated once before any is
generated a second time and the period will be c.

To produce a pseudo random sequence of integers in the range

$[0, n-1]$ we can generate a sequence $x_0, x_1, x_2, \ldots$ as suggested and then take as our random number

$$r_i = trunc\ (n*(x_i/c))$$

because x_i is an integer in the range $[0, c-1]$

and so x_i/c is a real in the range $[0, 1)$ $\{\geq 0$ and $<1\}$

and so $n*(x_i/c)$ is a real in the range $[0, n)$ $\{\geq 0$ and $<n\}$

and hence $trunc(n*(x_i/c))$ is an integer in the range $[0, n-1]$

```
PROGRAM DieTrials (input, output);

    (* The program simulates the throwing of a six-sided die
       until the same number appears on the top face on two
       successive throws.  By averaging over 100 trials, an
       estimate is produced of the number of attempts one
       might expect to make before achieving this. *)

    CONST
      a = 29;   b = 7;   c = 1024;
      nooftrials = 100;
      faces = 6;   minface = 1;

    VAR
      try, prev, thrown, x, noofthrows : integer;

BEGIN
    writeln ('Give me an integer in the range 0 to ', c-1 :1);
    readln (x);
    noofthrows := 0;

    FOR try := 1 TO nooftrials DO
    BEGIN
      noofthrows := noofthrows + 1;
      x := (a*x + b) MOD c;
      thrown := trunc (faces*(x/c)) + minface;
      REPEAT
        noofthrows := noofthrows + 1;   prev := thrown;
        x := (a*x + b) MOD c;
        thrown := trunc (faces*(x/c)) + minface
      UNTIL thrown = prev
    END;

    writeln ('Expected number of attempts to throw the same ');
    writeln ('number on two successive occasions is ',
                                 noofthrows/nooftrials :3:1)
  END.
```

Figure 7.9

The term x_i/c has been bracketed to ensure that division by c precedes multiplication by n. If the multiplication $n*x_i$ were performed first, integer overflow could occur if n is large.

To produce a pseudo random sequence of integers in the range [m,n] we can generate a sequence as before and then take

$$r_i = \text{trunc } ((n-m+1)*(x_i/c)) + m$$

The order of generation follows no obvious pattern and so the sequence can be regarded as effectively random. For best results, it is advisable to make p as large as possible and choose q to be approximately c/10 but, to be able to work in integers and avoid overflow, it is essential that

a(c-1)+b $\leq$ maxint

Thus, if maxint = 32767, sensible values are

p = 10   and   q = 3

giving

a = 29   b = 7   c = 1024   {a(c-1)+b = 29674}

Thus, to simulate a sequence of throws of a six-sided die, we could choose some value x in the range [0,1023] and then repeatedly obey the statement

x := (29*x + 7) MOD 1024

taking the values

trunc (6*(x/1024)) + 1

as the outcomes of successive throws.

The program of figure 7.9 does this to estimate (as the average of 100 trials) how many attempts one might expect to make before the same number is thrown on two successive attempts.

To generate a sequence of pseudo-random numbers with larger period, reals can be used in place of integers. The recurrence relation for x then becomes

$$y = ax_i + b$$
$$x_{i+1} = y - c*\text{trunc}(y/c)$$

with a, b, c, x_i, x_{i+1} and y now real. To produce a sequence of random numbers in the range [0,1), we would take

$$r_i = x_i/c$$

7.6 Exercises

*1. The equation

$$x^3 - 11x^2 - 10x - 24 = 0$$

has a solution that is a small positive integer. Write a program which finds a solution by trying in turn

x = 1, 2, 3, ...

*2. Write a program to produce the largest factor (other than n itself) of a given integer n.

3. If a real variable x initially has some value v and the value of x is repeatedly replaced by the value of

$$\frac{x + v/x}{2}$$

the values produced approach the square root of v.

Write a program which accepts as data a positive value v and uses the above technique to compute x such that

$$|x^2 - v| \leq 0.000001.$$

x is then an approximation to the square root of v. Your program should print the final value of x and state how many iterations are required to achieve the desired accuracy.

4. Write a program to compute the length of (ie the number of digits contained in) a given positive integer. The integer is to be introduced to the program as a user-defined constant.

*5. Given two distinct positive integers n and m such that n>m, the hcf (highest common factor) of m and n MOD m is the same as the hcf of n and m. Thus if we start with two positive values a and b, repeatedy replace the larger of the two by the appropriate modulo reduction, and stop when the modulo reduction gives 0, we have computed the hcf of a and b.
   Write a program to compute the hcf of two supplied integers.

*6.   (a) Extend your pocket calculator program for exercise 5.3.8 to accommodate expressions containing more than one operator (but no brackets) and terminated by an equals sign.
   (b) Further extend the program so that it displays the current answer whenever it meets an equals sign but continues to evaluate the expression until it meets some termination character of your choice. Your program should now also permit spaces to appear between an operand and an operator.

*7.   "Around the rugged rock,
           the ragged rascal ran.
           How many r's in that?
           Pray, tell me if you can."

           Write a program which can. Use any character of your choice to mark
           the end of the text.

  8. Write a program to count the number of words in a sentence assuming
     the sentence is terminated by a full stop and every word (including
     the last) is followed by at least one space or end of line.

  9. Extend your program of the previous exercise to accept a paragraph
     of text comprising one or more sentences and to compute the average
     sentence length. You may use any character of your choice to mark
     the end of a paragraph.

 10. Modify the loan repayment program of figure 6.6 to compute a
     repayment which, for a specified sum borrowed, leaves a final
     outstanding balance less than the monthly repayment (but not
     negative).

 11. Write a program to simulate the tossing of a coin. Use the program
     to estimate, as the average of 100 trials, the number of tosses one
     might expect to make before three successive tosses all produce
     'heads'.

 12. Write a program to simulate the successive cutting of a deck of
     playing cards, ignoring suits and considering only card
     denominations. Then modify the program to estimate, as the average
     of 50 trials, the number of cuts one might expect to make before
     the denomination revealed equals the number of the cut, counting
     cuts from 1 and returning to 1 after every thirteen cuts. Thus the
     program is estimating the number of cuts that are likely to be
     needed to produce an ace on the first cut (or fourteenth, or
     twenty-seventh, ...) or a deuce on the second cut (or fifteenth, or
     twenty-eighth, ...) and so on.

*13. The game 'last one loses' is played by two players and uses a pile
     of n counters, for some n. Players take turns and each turn entails
     removing 1, 2 or 3 counters from the pile. The game continues until
     there are no counters left and the winner is the one who does not
     take the last counter.
         Write a program to act as one player, playing at random until
     fewer than 5 counters remain (whereupon it is to play sensibly) and
     then play against your program.

CHAPTER 8
True or False?

In Pascal, every expression has an associated <u>type</u>. This includes a test following IF, WHILE or UNTIL and a test is considered to produce one of the two values "true" and "false". These are called <u>boolean values</u> and, consequently, a test is a particular case of a <u>boolean expression</u>. The data type "boolean" comprises only these two values and is an ordinal type. "false" has ordinal number 0 and "true" has ordinal number 1. Consequently "false" < "true". Boolean values can be written to a text file but not read from one.

8.1 Boolean case selector

A case-statement can emulate an if-statement. The test becomes a boolean selector and the two statements become limbs prefixed by "true" and "false".

```
CASE t OF
   true :  s1;
   false:  s2
END (* CASE *)
```

is equivalent to

```
IF t THEN s1 ELSE s2
```

The trailing ELSE problem of section 4.4 disappears if we replace one of the if-statements by a case-statement. The two forms presented at the end of section 4.4 become

```
CASE t1 OF
    true : IF t2 THEN s1;
    false : s2
END (* CASE *)
```

```
IF t1 THEN
CASE t2 OF
    true : s1;
    false : s2
END (* CASE *)
```

8.2 Boolean constants

A user-defined constant may have type boolean. A common use of user-defined boolean constants is to control the selection of output statements, particularly during the development of a program. As a check on the results produced by a quadratic equation solving program we might wish to produce extra output sometimes. For a quadratic equation

$$ax^2 + bx + c = 0$$

with two real roots u and v

$$u\ v\ =\ c/a$$
$$u\ +\ v\ =\ -b/a$$

The program of figure 8.1 assumes that the equation has real roots and, as well as printing the roots, prints their sum and product. This extra output is suppressed by simply redefining "sumandprodwanted" to be "false".

```
PROGRAM RealRoots (input, output);

      (* Solves a quadratic equation with
         real roots and offers steered output *)

   CONST
      sumandprodwanted = true;

   VAR
      a, b, c, x1, x2, rootofdisc : real;

BEGIN
   writeln ('Give me the coefficients of the equation');
   readln (a, b, c);

   rootofdisc := sqrt (sqr(b) - 4*a*c);
   x1 := (-b + rootofdisc) / (2*a);
   x2 := (-b - rootofdisc) / (2*a);

   writeln ('Roots are ', x1 :7:4, ' and ', x2 :7:4);

   IF sumandprodwanted THEN
   BEGIN
      writeln ('Sum of roots: ', x1 + x2 :7:4);
      writeln ('  -b/a : ', -b/a :7:4);   writeln;

      writeln ('Product of roots: ', x1 * x2 :7:4);
      writeln ('   c/a : ', c/a :7:4)
   END
END.
```

Figure 8.1

8.3 Boolean variables

A boolean variable can take either of the two values "true" and "false" and can acquire one of these values directly

```
   VAR
      b1, b2 : boolean;
    . . .
   b1 := true;   b2 := false;
```

or via a boolean expression.

```
VAR
    negative, posdisc, factorfound,
    spacenext, usersaysno, dhasreachedn : boolean;
    . . .
negative := digit < 0;
posdisc := disc > 0;
factorfound := n MOD d = 0;
spacenext := input^ = ' ';
usersaysno := reply = 'n';
dhasreachedn := d = n
```

In our program of figure 5.3 to print two three-letter words in alphabetical order, we can save some writing if we introduce a boolean variable. The program of figure 8.2 does this and is equivalent to the earlier version.

```
PROGRAM ThreeLetterWordsWithBooleanVariable (input, output);

    (* Prints two supplied three-letter
       words in alphabetical order *)

    VAR
        a1, a2, a3, b1, b2, b3 : char;
        abeforeb : boolean;

BEGIN
    writeln ('Type two three-letter words, one per line');
    readln (a1, a2, a3);   readln (b1, b2, b3);

    IF a1 < b1 THEN abeforeb := true ELSE
     IF a1 > b1 THEN abeforeb := false ELSE

      IF a2 < b2 THEN abeforeb := true ELSE
       IF a2 > b2 THEN abeforeb := false ELSE

         abeforeb := a3 <= b3;

    CASE abeforeb OF
      true : writeln (a1,a2,a3, ' ', b1,b2,b3);
      false : writeln (b1,b2,b3, ' ', a1,a2,a3)
    END (*CASE*)
END.
```

                        Figure 8.2

A boolean variable can be used to record the result of a test made within a loop. Reconsider the double letter detector of figure 7.5. The loop termination test is

```
input^ = space
```

and, within the loop, we make the test

        input^ = thisletter

If the letter test made within the loop is true, the space test used for
loop termination cannot possibly be. If we move the space test inside
the loop we can avoid making it if the letter test is true. We must then
keep a record of the termination test; we do this with a boolean
variable as in figure 8.3.

```
PROGRAM DoubleLettersWithBoolean (input, output);

    (* Counts the number of occurrences of
       double letters in a supplied word *)

    CONST
      space = ' ';

    VAR
      thisletter : char;
      doublecount : integer;
      spacemet : boolean;
BEGIN
    write ('What is your word? ');
    doublecount := 0;   spacemet := false;
    REPEAT
      read (thisletter);
      IF input^ = thisletter THEN
         doublecount := doublecount + 1
      ELSE
         spacemet := input^ = space
    UNTIL spacemet;

    writeln;
    writeln ('Number of double letters: ', doublecount :1)
END.
```

                        Figure 8.3

8.4 Boolean functions

There are three standard functions which produce a boolean result.

```
  odd  - detects an odd integer
  eof  - detects end of file
  eoln - detects end-of-line
```

8.4.1 <u>odd</u>

The expression

        odd (n)

delivers "true" if "n" is odd and "false" if "n" is even. We could have used this function in figure 6.5. The statement

        IF n MOD 2 = 0 THEN y := 1 ELSE y := x

becomes more transparent if written

        IF odd (n) THEN y := x ELSE y := 1

    We can use this function to improve the efficiency of our prime testing program of figure 7.2. We base our improvement upon the observation that an even number greater then two cannot be prime (because 2 is one of its factors). If n > 2, the search for a factor need be applied only if n is odd. Further, an odd number can have no even factors and so we need inspect only odd divisors. The improved program is in figure 8.4.

```
PROGRAM OddPrimeTester (input, output);

        (* Tests the primality of a supplied integer *)

    VAR
        d, n : integer;
        nisprime : boolean;

BEGIN
    write ('Give me an integer ');    readln (n);

    IF n < 2 THEN
        writeln ('   *** too small ***') ELSE
    BEGIN
        IF n = 2 THEN nisprime := true ELSE

            IF odd (n) THEN
            BEGIN
                d := 3;
                WHILE n MOD d <> 0 DO
                    d := d + 2;
                nisprime := d = n
            END ELSE
                nisprime := false;

        CASE nisprime OF
            true : writeln (n, ' is prime');
            false : writeln (n, ' is composite')
        END (* CASE *)
    END
END.
```

                    Figure 8.4

8.4.2 eoln

The end-of-line marker (which, you may recall, is a special space
character) can be detected using "eoln". The name of the file from which
the data is being read should be supplied as a parameter but, when it is
"input", the parameter may be omitted. Thus

            eoln (input)   and   eoln

are equivalent. They each deliver "true" if the character currently in
the input window is an end-of-line marker, and "false" otherwise.

The program of figure 8.5 counts the number of characters contained
in a supplied line of data. It does not count the end-of-line marker and
assumes that the line of data will contain at least one character in
addition to the end-of-line character.

```
      PROGRAM LineLength (input, output);

            (* Counts the number of characters in a
               line of data typed at the terminal *)

      VAR
          chcount : integer;

   BEGIN
      writeln ('Type a line of data');

      chcount := 0;
      REPEAT
          chcount := chcount + 1;    get (input)
      UNTIL eoln (input);

      writeln ('Line contains ', chcount :1, ' characters')
   END.
```

                        Figure 8.5

Now that we can recognise the end of a line we could relax the
constraint, in the program of figure 6.8, that students' names must be
the same length. To write a student's name to a file once a mark has
been read, we would simply copy the remainder of the line. For example,
the loop

```
      FOR chcount := 1 TO namelength DO
      BEGIN
          read (markfile, ch);   write (fails, ch)
      END
```

      would be replaced by

```
      REPEAT
          read (markfile, ch);   write (fails, ch)
      UNTIL eoln (markfile)
```

8.4.3 eof

The end of a data file can be detected with "eof". As with "eoln" any non-standard file must be specified as a parameter but "input" may be omitted. Thus

          eof (input)   and   eof

are equivalent. The program of figure 8.6 counts the number of lines in a text file "f" (but assumes that the file does contain at least one line).

```
     PROGRAM FileLength (f, output);

          (* Counts the lines in f *)

        VAR
           f : text;
           linecount : integer;

     BEGIN
        reset (f);    linecount := C;

        REPEAT
           linecount := linecount + 1;    readln (f)
        UNTIL eof (f);

        writeln (output, 'Number of lines in file: ', linecount :1)
     END.
```

                    Figure 8.6

     When cata is read from some device other than a terminal, the data file is completely prepared before the program is run. There is therefore an obvious end to the file. When data is supplied from a terminal, however, the situation is rather different. We do not type data until the program requests it and then it is read immediately so it might seem that we are nearly always at the end of the file. Alternatively, because we can always type more, it could be argued that we are never at the end of the file. Conseauently some terminal implementations of Pascal do not recognise the end of the standard file "input". Others may reserve a special control character which can be used to signify the end of the input. Check your particular implementation. We shall not apply "eof" to "input".

     The end of a text file can be detected only when the whole of the last line of the file has been read. When processing a text file, therefore, a call of "readln" should usually precede any test for the end of the file. It is therefore a simple matter to detect the end of the file when reading a sequence of numbers if the numbers are supplied one per line. As an example consider the program fragment of figure 7.8 to count and sum a sequence of examination marks, but with the modification that the file contains no data sentinel. We replace the test "mark<0" by

        eof (markfile)

and need take no steps to avoid treating a data sentinel as a mark. We now wish to process every number read so the fragment has the following form.

```
        reset (markfile);
        total := 0;    noofstudents := 0;
        REPEAT
           noofstudents := noofstudents + 1;
           readln (markfile, mark);    total := total + mark
        UNTIL eof (markfile)
```

The situation is not so straightforward however if several values may occupy one line. Consider a section of program to sum a sequence of integers supplied n per line in a file "f". We must read and sum n values using "read" and then call "readln" before testing "eof".

```
        reset (f);    sum := 0;
        REPEAT
           FOR i := 1 TO n DO
           BEGIN
              read (f, int);    sum := sum + int
           END;
           readln (f)
        UNTIL eof (f)
```

If several values may occupy one line but the number of values per line may vary, the situation becomes even more complicated. We tackle this in section 8.6.

Even when processing characters it is a good idea to arrange for a call of "eof" to follow a call of "readln". The following program fragment will process each line of a file on a character-by-character basis.

```
        VAR
           f : text;    ch : char;
         . . .
        reset (f);
        REPEAT
           REPEAT
              read (f,ch);    ...
           UNTIL eoln (f);
           readln (f)
        UNTIL eof (f)
```

8.5 Boolean operators

If a boolean expression is preceded by the operator

        NOT

its value is <u>inverted</u>. If "b" has the value "true" then "NOT b" is "false"; if "b" has the value "false" then "NOT b" is "true".

If we were to modify the program of figure 8.5 to cater for a line of data which contains only the end-of-line character we would want to replace the repeat-loop by a while-loop. The continuation condition for the while-loop is that the end of the line has <u>not</u> been reached.

```
chcount := 0;
WHILE NOT eoln (input) DO
BEGIN
    chcount := chcount + 1;    get (input)
END;
```

In much the same way that arithmetic operands are combined using * and +, so boolean operands can be combined using two boolean operators

```
AND

OR
```

If b1 and b2 are booleans

b1 AND b2   is "true" only if b1 <u>and</u> b2 are both "true"

b1 OR b2   is "true" if either b1 <u>or</u> b2 is "true"
                              (or both are true)

Each of these operators has a different precedence. Their precedence <u>decreases</u> in the order

```
NOT    { highest precedence }
AND    { same precedence as DIV MOD * / }
OR     { same precedence as + - }
```

In chapter 4 we looked at ways to check the validity of the data supplied to the digit naming program of figure 4.3. One way to check that an integer lies between two bounds is by using AND.

```
IF (digit >= 1) AND (digit <= 9) THEN
    . . .
ELSE
    writeln ('Digit out of range')
```

If we inverted the test we would use OR.

```
IF (digit < 1) OR (digit > 9) THEN
    writeln ('Digit out of range')
ELSE
    . . .
```

This example illustrates an application of "de Morgan's Law", an important theorem of boolean algebra. To invert a test

```
a AND b
```

we can replace AND by OR and invert both a and b. Thus

        NOT (a AND b) = a' OR b'

where a' = NOT a and b' = NOT b. Similarly

        NOT (a OR b) = a' AND b'.

     A sequence of boolean expressions can be strung together in much
the same way as can a sequence of arithmetic expressions. Recall the
naming program of figure 5.2 for Amanda and her friends. The program
fails if any initial other than A, B, C or F is supplied. We can check
for this. Here are two possibilities.

        IF (initial = 'A') OR (initial = 'B') OR
           (initial = 'C') OR (initial = 'F') THEN ...

        IF (initial >= 'A') AND (initial <= 'F') AND
           NOT ((initial ='D') OR (initial = 'E')) THEN ...

All the brackets are necessary because of the relative priorities of the
operators involved. For example, if no brackets appeared in the second
form, it would be interpreted as

        IF initial >= ('A' AND initial) <= ('F' AND
           (NOT initial)) = ('D' OR initial) = 'E' THEN ...

and this is nonsense!

8.6 Multi-exit loops

Each non-deterministic loop encountered so far has had only one reason
for exit. Apart from a possible appearance of NOT the loop test has
involved only a boolean variable, a boolean function call or a simple
comparison of two operands:

            input^ = space   { Figures 7.1, 7.3, 7.4, 7.5 }
            n MOD d <> 0   { Figures 7.2, 8.4 }
            thisterm > bound   { Figure 7.6 }
            reply = 'n'   { Figure 7.7 }
            mark < 0   { Figure 7.8 }
            thrown = prev   { Figure 7.9 }
            spacemet   { Figure 8.3 }
            eoln (input)   { Figure 8.5 }
            NOT eof(f)   { Figure 8.6 }

We often wish to terminate a loop for any of several reasons. This can
happen if we further improve the efficiency of our prime testing program
of figure 8.4.

     A composite number has at least one factor which does not exceed
its square root. Consequently, we can terminate the search for a factor
of n when we reach the square root of n. We therefore wish to terminate
the loop when

          (n MOD d = 0) OR (d >= sqrt(n))

and then declare n to be prime only if

          n MOD d <> 0

The full program is in figure 8.7.

```
    PROGRAM PrimeTester (input, output);

        (* Tests the primality of a supplied integer *)

        VAR
          d, n, rootofn : integer;
          nisprime : boolean;

   BEGIN
       write ('Give me an integer ');    readln (n);

       IF n < 2 THEN
           writeln ('   *** too small ***') ELSE
       BEGIN
          IF n = 2 THEN nisprime := true ELSE

             IF odd (n) THEN
             BEGIN
                rootofn := round (sqrt (n));
                d := 3;
                WHILE (n MOD d <> 0) AND (d < rootofn) DO
                    d := d + 2;
                nisprime := n MOD d <> 0
             END ELSE
                nisprime := false;

          CASE nisprime OF
             true : writeln (n, ' is prime');
             false : writeln (n, ' is composite')
          END (* CASE *)
       END
   END.
```

                       Figure 8.7

Notice that, upon exit from the loop we must test (n MOD d <> 0) and not
(d < rootofn) because (d < rootofn) can be false whether n is prime or
not. For example, if n=49 (composite) the process will terminate with
d=7 (and so d = rootofn) and if n=47 (prime) the process will terminate
with d=7 (and so d > rootofn). For this reason, the test (n MOD d <> 0)
is called the dominant test; the other test (d < rootofn) is an
auxiliary test - it is not a fundamental part of the prime detection
mechanism, it is merely there to speed up the process.

    Figure 8.3 illustrated the use of a boolean variable to record the
outcome of a termination test made within a loop. This technique can

improve the transparency of a loop with a complicated termination test
such as we have in figure 8.7. We make both termination tests within the
loop and record the result of each with a boolean variable. The loop
body becomes

```
d := d + 2;
factorfound := n MOD d = 0;
rootreached := d >= rootofn
```

assuming we have declared two boolean variables "factorfound" and
"rootreached".

If we use a while-loop it will have the form

```
WHILE NOT (factorfound OR rootreached) DO
```

and so the two boolean variables will have to be initialized before the
loop is entered. If we use a repeat-loop, however, it will have the form

```
REPEAT
    . . .
UNTIL factorfound OR rootexceeded
```

and the boolean variables will acquire values within the loop body
before the termination test is made. There is then no need to initialize
the variables prior to loop entry. Inspection of figure 8.7 shows that
the first loop test must be made for d=3. If we use a repeat-loop with
the body suggested, we must initialize "d" to 1 before the loop is
entered. This value will be incremented to 3 before the boolean
variables record the outcomes of the tests. The final program is in
figure 8.8. Notice that the role of the boolean variable "nisprime" of
figure 8.7 is now served by "factorfound" (which implies the opposite
condition).

Rather than use two boolean variables we might decide to use only
one. If so, this must be the one recording the dominant condition –
"factorfound". The loop becomes

```
REPEAT
    d := d + 2;
    factorfound := n MOD d = 0
UNTIL factorfound OR (d >= rootofn)
```

In this example we have a choice whether or not to involve variables to
record the outcomes of termination tests. This is because the two tests
are independent. The truth (or falsity) of one does not affect the
validity of the other. If two tests are dependent we have no choice; we
must record at least one outcome within the loop. This is the case with
the situation outlined at the end of section 8.4 where we wish to form
the sum of a number of integers stored in a text file "f" but several
integers may occupy one line and the number per line may vary.

Because we do not know how many values occupy a line we must read
them with "read" and not "readln". As a first approximation we can write

```
reset (f);   sum := 0;
REPEAT
    read (f, int);   sum := sum + int
UNTIL eof (f)
```

```
     PROGRAM PrimeWithBooleans (input, output);

          (* Tests the primality of a supplied integer *)

       VAR
          d, n, rootofn : integer;
          factorfound, rootreached : boolean;

   BEGIN
       write ('Give me an integer ');   readln (n);

       IF n < 2 THEN
          writeln ('   *** too small ***') ELSE
       BEGIN
          IF n = 2 THEN factorfound := false ELSE

             IF odd (n) THEN
             BEGIN
                rootofn := round (sqrt (n));
                d := 1;
                REPEAT
                   d := d + 2;
                   factorfound := n MOD d = 0;
                   rootreached := d >= rootofn
                UNTIL factorfound OR rootreached
             END ELSE
                factorfound := true;

          CASE factorfound OF
             true : writeln (n, ' is composite');
             false : writeln (n, ' is prime')
          END (* CASE *)
       END
   END.
```

                          Figure 8.8

---

but this will not work because "eof(f)" cannot be true immediately after
an integer has been read by "read" even when the last integer in the
file has been read. The file will still contain at least the end-of-line
marker of the last line. To overcome this we follow the call of "read"
by a loop to skip subsequent spaces until a non-space character is
encountered or the end of the file is reached, whichever is the sooner.
This suggests that the earlier program fragment might become

```
          reset (f);   sum := 0;
          REPEAT
             read (f, int);   sum := sum + int;
             REPEAT
                get (f)
             UNTIL (f^ <> space) OR eof (f)
          UNTIL eof (f)
```

Unfortunately, this still doesn't work! The problem lies with the inner
loop termination test

```
        (f^ <> space) OR eof (f)
```
and stems from the fact that its two constituents are not independent.
If "eof(f)" is true, "f^" is undefined and then an attempt to evaluate
(f^ <> space) generates an execution error. We must ensure that the test
"eof(f)" is made <u>first</u> and the test (f^ <> space) made only if "eof(f)"
is false. This means that we <u>must</u> make the tests <u>inside</u> the loop and we
<u>must</u> record the outcome of the test (f^ <> space). The final solution is
shown in figure 8.9 and uses boolean variables to record the outcomes of
both tests.

     In other programming languages, boolean variables play an important
role in this context. We shall see in chapter 11 that Pascal provides a
better alternative which we shall usually adopt in subsequent multi-exit
loops.

```
    VAR
        f : text;
        sum, int : integer;
        spacenext, atfileend : boolean;

     . . .

    reset (f);   sum := 0;
    REPEAT
        read (f, int);   sum := sum + int;
        spacenext := false;   atfileend := false;
        REPEAT
            get (f);
            IF eof (f) THEN atfileend := true ELSE
                spacenext := f^ = space
        UNTIL atfileend OR NOT spacenext
    UNTIL atfileend
```

                          Figure 8.9

8.7 Set membership

Pascal allows the construction of <u>sets</u>. Square brackets, [and], are
used as <u>set constructors</u> and members are separated by commas. All
members of a set must have the same type, and this must be an ordinal
type (and, hence, not "real"). This is called the <u>base type</u> of the set.
A set member may be represented by any expression of the base type. Here
are some examples

```
        [1, 2, 3, 5, 7, 11]              { set of integers }
        ['a', 'e' 'i' 'o', 'u']          { set of characters }
        [i+1, ord(input^), ord('A')-1]   { set of integers }
```

     A shorthand notation is available for a contiguous group of set
members. The set

          [4, i-2, i, 6, i+1, i-1, i-4, i+3, 5, i+2]

can be written

          [4 .. 6, i-2 .. i+3, i-4]

    Multiple occurrences of a value are equivalent to a single
occurrence of that value. The set

          ['C'..'H', 'W', 'E', 'F'..'K', succ(input^)]

is the set

          ['C'..'K', 'W', succ(input^)]

    Set membership can be detected with the relational operator

          IN

The right hand operand must be a set and the left hand operand must be
an expression whose type is the same as the base type of the set. The
operator yields "true" only if the value of the left hand operand is
currently a member of the right hand set.

    The best way for Amanda and her friends to guard against
inappropriate initials is to use a set:

          IF initial IN ['A'..'C', 'F'] THEN ...

    The best way to check that an integer is in the range 1 to 9 is
with a set.

          IF digit IN [1 .. 9] THEN ...

    Consider now a program fragment to compute the length of a supplied
word. The word may contain hyphens and apostrophes and must start with a
capital letter but any other letters will be lower case. Any non-
alphabetic characters preceding the word are to be skipped. The overall
process comprises two steps

          Skip to word
          Determine word length

Skipping to a word entails skipping characters until we reach a letter.
There may be no characters to be skipped so we need a while-loop.

          WHILE NOT (input^ IN ['A'..'Z', 'a'..'z']) DO
             get (input)

    To determine the word length we must get to the other end of the
word and count how many characters we have to skip to get there. There
must be at least one character so we use a repeat-loop.

```
length := 0;
REPEAT
    length := length + 1;   get (input)
UNTIL NOT (input^ IN ['a'..'z', '-', ''''])
```

One final note: sets are <u>implementation dependent</u>. Both the maximum size of a set and the range of ordinal numbers that set members may possess vary from one computer to another. Most restrict the maximum ordinal number to something fairly small (typically 64 or 128) and few accommodate negative integers. It is possible, therefore, that the program fragment immediately above may not be accepted by some compilers.

8.8 Exercises

*1. Introduce a boolean variable to your program for exercise 4.5.11 to record whether the person has had a birthday this year. The program is then to use this information to determine the person's age.

2. Modify your program for exercise 7.6.8 to recgnise a full stop, question mark or exclamation mark as the end of a sentence. Do this by introducing a boolean variable "endmet", initially set false but then set true if any one of the three terminators is encountered. You should test for each terminator in turn.

*3. (a) Write a program to copy a text file. The program is to generate one file as an exact copy of another.
    (b) Modify the program so that, in the output file, any group of successive spaces has been reduced to a single space. You may assume that a space will never immediately precede an end-of-line marker.

4. A text file contains an alphabetically ordered list of surnames, typed one per line. Write a program to determine the most frequently occurring surname initial.

5. Write a program which reads from a file a series of temperature readings in the range -20 to 40 and plots them graphically with the average displayed as a vertical axis. The first few lines of output might have the following form.

```
1                         +*
2                         +  *
3                         +  *
4                         *
5                         *+
6                         *  +
```

The distance of a '*' from the line number indicates a temperature reading and the position of each '+' indicates the average for the whole period.

6. Write a program to state whether three supplied letters are in alphabetical order.

*7. Write a program to determine whether a given five-letter word is palindromic. A palindrome reads the same backwards and forwards.

*8. Introduce a boolean variable to your program for exercise 7.6.13 to indicate whether it is the machine's turn to play or the opponent's. The main part of the program should then be a loop which repeatedly inverts the value of this variable.

*9. Write a program to accept an integer and the bounds of two (possibly overlapping) integer ranges and to classify the integer as
>   in neither range,
>   in the first range only,
>   in the second range only, or
>   in both ranges.
Your program is to test whether the integer is in the first range once only and in the second range once only.

*10. A data file contains 365 values representing the rainfall in millimetres for consecutive days in a year. Write a program which counts how many days have elapsed before the total rainfall for the year exceeds 250 millimetres. Allow for the possibility of a very dry year.

11. Modify your program for exercise 7.6.12 to estimate the number of cuts one might expect to make before three successive cuts produce three ascending (but not necessarily consecutive) denominations.

12. The game 'one is zero' is for two or more players and is played with a six-sided die as follows. All players start with a zero score and take turns. At each turn a player throws the die until either he chooses to finish his turn or he throws a '1' (whichever is the sooner). If he stops before throwing a '1', all the numbers thrown are added to his score; if he throws a '1', no points are added to his score. A game consists of ten turns for each player and, at the end of the game, the player with the highest score wins. Consider the following two questions.

(i) If a player always attempts to make n throws and then finish his turn after the nth throw, what is a good value for n?

(ii) If a player always attempts to score at least p points and then finish his turn as soon as at least p points have been scored during that turn, what is a good value for p?

To answer the first question, write a program that simulates five games for each of n = 1, 2, 3, ..., 25 and prints the average score obtained for each value of n. To answer the second question, first write a program that simulates five games for each of p = 5, 10, 15, 20, ..., 100 to find a good 'region' [p1,p2] for p; then run the program to simulate five games for each of p = p1, p1+1, ..., p2.

13. Write a program to count the number of words in a sentence. Words
    are to contain letters and, possibly, hyphens and apostrophes and
    words are separated by at least one space or end-of-line and,
    possibly, a comma, colon or semi-colon. The end of the sentence is
    indicated by a full stop, exclamation mark or question mark
    immediately following the last word. Rather than adopt the approach
    of exercise 2, you are to use sets.

14. Extend your program for exercise 13 to count the average number of
    words per sentence in a paragraph of text. The paragraph is stored
    in a text file and no data sentinel heralds its end.

CHAPTER 9
A Matter of Routine

Procedures and functions are called <u>routines</u>. A routine is essentially a small piece of program with an associated name. Routines offer two benefits. Transparency is improved when the purpose of a group of statements is indicated by a single name. Duplication is avoided when one routine is <u>called</u> several times.

A procedure is a routine which causes some change. A function is a routine which causes no change but computes a value. Consequently, a procedure call constitutes a statement whereas a function call constitutes an expression.

We have already met some standard procedures (write, writeln, read, readln, get, put) and functions (sin, cos, sqrt, odd, eoln, ...). Pascal allows us to extend the number of routines available by declaring our own. They must be declared between the variable declarations (if there are any) and the BEGIN of the program body.

9.1 Procedures

A simple procedure has the basic form

```
PROCEDURE p;
BEGIN
    s_1; s_2; ...; s_n
END (* p *) ;

where   p is the procedure name

and     s_1, s_2, ..., s_n are statements
```

The statements $s_1, ..., s_n$ constitute the <u>procedure body</u>. The procedure can be <u>called</u> from the main program by simply quoting its name. This gives a <u>procedure call</u> statement. When a procedure is called, the statements of the procedure body are obeyed and then control returns to the statement following the call.

On a number of occasions we have defined an algorithm as a sequence of named actions and then expanded these. For example, in chapter 8, we derived a program fragment to count the number of characters in a word contained somewhere in a line of text. There were two named actions

Skip to word
Determine word length

and each expanded to a loop. A complete program might have the following structure.

```
        Give prompt
        Skip to word
        Determine word lengt
        State word Length
```

Rather than replace these actions by their expansions we can declare them as procedures. As with program names, we include upper case letters within procedure names. The program has the form shown in figure 9.1.

```
    PROGRAM WordLength (input, output);

        (* Determines length of a supplied word *)

    VAR
        Length : integer;

    PROCEDURE DetermineWordLength;
    BEGIN
        length := 0;
        REPEAT
            length := length + 1;    get (input)
        UNTIL NOT (input^ IN ['a'..'z', '-', ''''])
    END (* Determine word length *) ;

    PROCEDURE GivePrompt;
    BEGIN
        writeln ('Type a line containing a word')
    END (* Give prompt *) ;

    PROCEDURE SkipToWord;
    BEGIN
        WHILE NOT (input^ IN ['A'..'Z', 'a'..'z']) DO
            get (input)
    END (* Skip to word *) ;

    PROCEDURE StateWordLength;
    BEGIN
        writeln ('Word contains', length :1, ' characters')
    END (* State word length *) ;

  BEGIN (* program body *)
      GivePrompt;    SkipToWord;
      DetermineWordLength;    StateWordLength
  END.
```

Figure 9.1

Program transparency has been improved. The intent of the program body is more readily apparent. Procedures provide a useful means of distinguishing the different <u>logic levels</u> of a program. The <u>top</u> level of program logic is defined in the program body. The statements which

achieve these activities named at the top level constitute a <u>lower</u> level
of program logic.

We now reconsider the program of figure 6.8 to process a file of
examination marks, but with modifications suggested in chapter 8; the
length of each name is unknown, the number of marks provided is unknown
and the file contains no data sentinel.

We decided the structure of the program would be

        Compute top mark and average
        List top mark holders and failures

and then expanded these two activities to produce the final program
body. In the program of figure 9.2 each has been written as a procedure.

```
PROGRAM ExamMarks (markfile, tops, fails);

    (* Processes a file of examination marks *)

VAR
    markfile, tops, fails : text;
    noofstudents, topcount, failcount, total,
      mark, topmark, passmark, stud : integer;
    average : real;
    ch : char;

PROCEDURE ComputeTopAndAverage;
BEGIN
    reset (markfile);    noofstudents := 0;
    topmark := 0;    total := 0;
    REPEAT
       noofstudents := noofstudents + 1;
       readln (markfile, mark);    total := total + mark;
       IF mark > topmark THEN
           topmark := mark
    UNTIL eof (markfile);
    average := total / noofstudents
END  (* Compute top and average *) ;

PROCEDURE ListTopsAndFails;
BEGIN
    rewrite (tops);    rewrite (fails);
    writeln (tops, 'Number of candidates: ', noofstudents :1);
    writeln (fails, 'Number of candidates: ', noofstudents :1);

    writeln (tops, 'Average mark: ', average :4:1);
    writeln (fails, 'Average mark: ', average :4:1);

    writeln (tops, 'Highest mark: ', topmark :1);
    writeln (tops);
    writeln (tops, 'Candidates with highest mark:');
```

```
         passmark := trunc (2 * average / 3);
         writeln (fails, 'Pass mark: ', passmark :1);
         writeln (fails);
         writeln (fails, 'Candidates below pass mark:');

         reset (markfile);
         topcount := 0;   failcount := 0;
         FOR stud := 1 TO noofstudents DO
         BEGIN
            read (markfile, mark);
            IF mark < passmark THEN
            BEGIN
               failcount := failcount + 1;
               REPEAT
                  read (markfile, ch);   write (fails, ch)
               UNTIL eoln (markfile);
               writeln (fails)
            END ELSE
               IF mark = topmark THEN
               BEGIN
                  topcount := topcount + 1;
                  REPEAT
                     read (markfile, ch);   write (tops, ch)
                  UNTIL eoln (markfile);
                  writeln (tops)
               END;
            readln (markfile)
         END;

         writeln (tops);
         writeln (tops, 'Number of candidates: ', topcount :1);
         writeln (fails);
         writeln (fails, 'Number of candidates: ', failcount :1)
      END  (* List tops and fails *) ;

   BEGIN  (* program body *)
      ComputeTopAndAverage;   ListTopsAndFails
   END.
```

Figure 9.2

One procedure may call another. A procedure may even call itself. It is then said to display <u>recursion</u> but this is beyond the scope of the current book. The only restriction is that the declaration of a procedure must precede its calls. Within the procedure "ListTopsAndFails" we might decide to use procedures to copy students' names to the output files and to generate the headings for the two lists of names. The form of the procedure "ListTopsAndFails" can be as in figure 9.3 if we introduce the other three procedures shown. The declaration of "ListTopsAndFails" must come <u>after</u> the declarations of "CopyToFails", "CopyToTops" and "Headings" (but we shall relax this constraint later).

```
PROCEDURE CopyToFails;
BEGIN
   REPEAT
      read (markfile, ch);    write (fails, ch)
   UNTIL eoln (markfile);
   writeln (fails)
END  (* Copy to fails *) ;

PROCEDURE CopyToTops;
BEGIN
   REPEAT
      read (markfile, ch);    write (tops, ch)
   UNTIL eoln (markfile);
   writeln (tops)
END  (* Copy to tops *) ;

PROCEDURE Headings;
BEGIN
   rewrite (tops);    rewrite (fails);
   writeln (tops, 'Number of candidates: ', noofstudents :1);
   writeln (fails, 'Number of candidates: ', noofstudents :1);

   writeln (tops, 'Average mark: ', average :4:1);
   writeln (fails, 'Average mark: ', average :4:1);

   writeln (tops, 'Highest mark: ', topmark :1);
   writeln (tops);
   writeln (tops, 'Candidates with highest mark:');

   writeln (fails, 'Pass mark: ', passmark :1);
   writeln (fails);
   writeln (fails, 'Candidates below pass mark:')
END  (* Headings *) ;

PROCEDURE ListTopsAndFails;
BEGIN
   passmark := trunc (2 * average / 3);
   Headings;
   reset (markfile);
   topcount := 0;    failcount := 0;
   FOR stud := 1 TO noofstudents DO
   BEGIN
      read (markfile, mark);
      IF mark < passmark THEN
      BEGIN
         failcount := failcount + 1;
         CopyToFails
      END ELSE
         IF mark = topmark THEN
         BEGIN
            topcount := topcount + 1;
            CopyToTops
         END;
```

```
        readln (markfile)
    END;

    writeln (tops);
    writeln (tops, 'Number of candidates: ', topcount :1);
    writeln (fails);
    writeln (fails, 'Number of candidates: ', failcount :1)
  END (* List tops and fails *) ;
```

                          Figure 9.3

9.2 Localized information

You must have noticed a similarity between a procedure body and a
program body. Each contains a sequence of statements (presented as a
compound statement) which may refer to entities declared 'outside'. The
procedures in figures 9.1 and 9.2 refer to identifiers defined in the
main program just as statements within the program body can refer to
"read", "write", "maxint", "integer" etc.

    This similarity extends. A program can contain declarations
specifying entities which may be used by procedures which are declared
within the program and by the statements of the program body. The same
applies to procedures. A procedure declaration may contain its own
declarations. Any entity declared within a procedure may be used by any
procedure declared within the procedure and by the statements of the
procedure body. Declarations within a procedure appear between the
PROCEDURE line and the BEGIN of the procedure body and are subject to
the same rules of order as in the main program.

    The main program and each procedure constitutes a block. An entity
does not exist outside the block in which it is declared: its scope
extends from its point of definition to the end of the most locally
enclosing block. An entity declared within a procedure is said to be
local to that procedure. An entity declared in the main program is said
to be global. Storage space for local variables is allocated at run-time
when a block is entered and released when the block is exited. So, even
if two variables in different blocks have the same name, they will refer
to different storage locations at run-time.

    It is good practice to declare variables as locally as possible.
This reduces the possibility of their corruption in other parts of the
program. Let us see how we can localize information within our
examination mark program in its current form with five procedures.

    The procedure "ComputeTopAndAverage" uses two variables which have
nothing to do with the rest of the program. The variable "total" is not
used outside this procedure. The variable "mark" is used outside this
procedure but need not be. Within this procedure we could replace it by
a new variable and the function of the program would not change. We
effectively do this if we make it local to the procedure. We remove
these two variables from the global declarations and define them within
the procedure:

```
        PROCEDURE Compute Top And Average;
            VAR
                mark, total : integer;
        BEGIN
            . . .        { as in figure 9.2 }
        END  (* Compute top and average *) ;
```

The procedure "CopyToTops" uses a variable, "ch", which has nothing to do with the rest of the program. The procedure "CopyToFails" uses a variable, called "ch", but it has nothing to do with any variable used within "CopyToTops". It could be given a different name within one procedure and the effect of the program would be unchanged. Each of these two procedures should therefore have its own copy of "ch". We remove "ch" from the global declarations and declare it inside both of the copying procedures.

```
        PROCEDURE CopyToFails;
            VAR
                ch : char;
        BEGIN
            . . .        { as in figure 9.3 }
        END  (* Copy to fails *) ;

        PROCEDURE CopyToTops;
            VAR
                ch : char;
        BEGIN
            . . .        { as in figure 9.3 }
        END  (* Copy to tops *) ;
```

None of the variables referred to inside the procedure "Headings" can be made local.

By an argument similar to that applied to "ComputeTopAndAverage", the procedure "ListTopsAndFails" requires its own copies of "mark" and "stud". Indeed, the Pascal Standard insists that a for-loop control variable be declared locally so we <u>must</u> declare "stud" locally. The three variables "passmark", "topcount" and "failcount" are needed by both "ListTopsAndFails" and "Headings". However, the procedure "Headings" is not used outside the body of "ListTopsAndFails" and so it should be declared inside "ListTopsAndFails". The three variables "passmark", "topcount" and "failcount" can then be made local to "ListTopsAndFails" because they will still be in scope when the procedure "Headings" is declared. The procedures "CopyToTops" and "CopyToFails" are called only within "ListTopsAndFails" and so they too should be made local. The resulting declaration structure of the program is shown in figure 9.4. Notice that the only global entities are now the text files and the three variables to which both the top-level procedures refer.

9.3 Functions

The fundamental difference between a function and a procedure is that a function call constitutes an <u>expression</u> because a function <u>delivers</u> a <u>result</u> whereas a procedure call constitutes a <u>statement</u> and no value is associated with the call.

```
PROGRAM ExamMarks (markfile, tops, fails);

    (* Processes a file of examination marks *)

VAR
   markfile, tops, fails : text;
   noofstudents, topmark : integer;
   average : real;

PROCEDURE ComputeTopAndAverage;
   VAR
      mark, total, stud : integer;
BEGIN
   . . .      { as in figure 9.2 }
END  (* Compute top and ave *) ;

PROCEDURE ListTopsAndFails;
   VAR
      mark, passmark, stud, topcount, failcount : integer;

   PROCEDURE CopyToFails;
      VAR
         ch : char;
   BEGIN
      . . .      { as in figure 9.3 }
   END  (* Copy to fails *) ;

   PROCEDURE CopyToTops;
      VAR
         ch : char;
   BEGIN
      . . .      { as in figure 9.3 }
   END  (* Copy to tops *) ;

   PROCEDURE Headings;
   BEGIN
      . . .      { as in figure 9.3 }
   END (* Headings *) ;

BEGIN  (* List tops and fails *)
   . . .      { as in figure 9.3 }
END  (* List tops and fails *) ;

BEGIN  (* program body *)
   ComputeTopAndAverage;  ListTopsAndFails
END.
```

Figure 9.4

A function is a suitable form for a routine when we are interested
in only one value computed by the routine and the routine produces no
side effects. A routine is said to cause a side effect if it produces

any non-local change. All the procedures we have met in this chapter
have side effects. A function with side effects is undesirable because
functions are used in expressions and a program can be hard to follow if
evaluation of an expression causes non-local changes.

In Pascal, a function may deliver a result of any ordinal type
(boolean, char, integer, symbolic, subrange), of type real or of any
pointer type. Symbolic and subrange types are discussed in chapter 11
and pointer types are beyond the scope of the current book. A function
declaration differs from a procedure declaration in three respects.

1. FUNCTION replaces PROCEDURE.

2. The type of the result delivered by the function is quoted
(preceded by a colon) before the closing semicolon of the function
heading.

3. Within the function body, there must be at least one assignment
statement with the function identifier on the left hand side.

```
PROGRAM RaiseToKnownPowerWithFn (input, output);

    (* Raises a number x to an integer power n *)

    VAR
        x : real;
        n : integer;

    FUNCTION xtothen : real;
        VAR
            xsquared, p : real;
            power : integer;
    BEGIN
        IF n = 0 THEN xtothen := 1 ELSE
        BEGIN
            xsquared := sqr (x);
            IF odd (n) THEN p := x ELSE p := 1;
            FOR power := 1 TO n DIV 2 DO
                p := p * xsquared;
            xtothen := p
        END
    END  (* x to the n *) ;

BEGIN  (* program body *)
    write ('Please give me a number ');   readln (x);
    write ('To what power would you like it raised? ');
    readln (n);
    writeln (x, ' raised to the power ', n :1, ' is ', xtothen)
END.
```

Figure 9.5

```
PROGRAM PrimeWithFn (input, output);

    (* Tests the primality of a supplied integer *)

   VAR
      n : integer;

   FUNCTION nisprime : boolean;
      VAR
         rootofn, d : integer;
         factorfound : boolean;
   BEGIN
      IF n = 2 THEN nisprime := true ELSE
         IF odd (n) THEN
         BEGIN
            rootofn := round (sqrt (n));
            d := 1;
            REPEAT
               d := d + 2;    factorfound := n MOD d = 0
            UNTIL factorfound OR (d >= rootofn);
            nisprime := NOT factorfound
         END ELSE
            nisprime := false
   END  (* n is prime *) ;

BEGIN  (* program body *)
   write ('Give me an integer ');    readln (n);
   IF n < 2 THEN writeln ('   *** too small ***') ELSE
   CASE nisprime OF
      true : writeln (n, ' is prime');
      false : writeln (n, ' is composite')
   END (* CASE *)
END.
```

Figure 9.6

We have seen situations suitable for functions in the programs to raise a number to a specified power (figures 6.4 and 6.5), the various prime testing programs (figures 7.2, 8.4, 8.7 and 8.8) and in the programs of figures 4.5 ("InsuranceGrouping"), 7.6 ("MinFib") and 8.2 ("ThreeLetterWordsWithABooleanVariable").

If the process of raising a number to a power were written as a function, the program of figure 6.5 might take the form shown in figure 9.5.

We use a function name on the left hand side of an assignment statement when we wish to give a value to the function but a function reference in almost any other context constitutes a function call. The only exception to this is when a function name is passed as an actual parameter (corresponding to a formal function) as described in section 10.3. In our powering function we must maintain a local variable ("p") to compute the result within the loop. If we were to remove the declaration of "p" and replace the occurrence of "p" within the loop by "xtothen", the loop body would be

        xtothen := xtothen * xsquared

and this would not work. The function reference on the right hand side constitutes a recursive function call (not covered in the current book).

A function to determine whether a given integer is prime delivers a boolean value and the program of figure 8.8, using such a function, could be as in figure 9.6.

A function to produce the insurance group appropriate for a given age, as in figure 4.5, delivers a character (one of the letters A, B, C, D) and the program of figure 4.5, modified to include such a function, would have the form shown in figure 9.7.

```
PROGRAM InsuranceGroupWithFn (input, output);

    (* Categorizes an age
       into one of four groups *)

    VAR
       age : integer;

    FUNCTION groupforage : char;
    BEGIN
       CASE age DIV 5 OF
          3          : groupforage := 'A';
          4, 5       : groupforage := 'B';
          6, 7, 8, 9 : groupforage := 'C';
          10,11,12   : groupforage := 'D'
       END (* CASE *)
    END  (* group for age *) ;

 BEGIN (* program body *)
    write ('Supply an age ');   readln (age);
    writeln ('Insurance group is ', groupforage)
 END.
```

Figure 9.7

A function to produce the smallest Fibanacci number above a specified bound delivers an integer and so the program of figure 7.6, using a function, would have the form shown in figure 9.8. The only variable needed by the program body is "bound"; the others have therefore become local to the function.

A function to determine whether two three-letter words are supplied in alphabetical order delivers a boolean value and figure 9.9 shows the program of figure 8.2, modified to incorporate such a function.

```
PROGRAM MinFibWithFn (input, output);

    (* Computes the smallest Fibonacci
       number which exceeds a specified bound *)

VAR
   bound : integer;

FUNCTION minfiboverbound : integer;
   VAR
      thisterm, prevterm, termbeforethat : integer;
BEGIN
   thisterm := 1;   prevterm := 0;
   REPEAT
      termbeforethat := prevterm;   prevterm := thisterm;
      thisterm := prevterm + termbeforethat
   UNTIL thisterm > bound;
   minfiboverbound := thisterm
END  (* min fib over bound *) ;

BEGIN  (* program body *)
   write ('Specify a bound ');   readln (bound);
   IF bound < 1 THEN
      writeln ('   *** bound is too small ***')
   ELSE
      writeln ('Smallest Fibonacci number greater than ',
              bound :1, ' is ', minfiboverbound :1)
END.
```

Figure 9.8

```
PROGRAM ThreeLetterWordsWithFn (input, output);

    (* Prints two supplied three-letter
       words in alphabetical order *)

VAR
   a1, a2, a3, b1, b2, b3 : char;

FUNCTION abinorder : boolean;
BEGIN
   IF a1 < b1 THEN abinorder := true ELSE
    IF a1 > b1 THEN abinorder := false ELSE
       IF a2 < b2 THEN abinorder := true ELSE
        IF a2 > b2 THEN abinorder := false ELSE
           abinorder := a3 <= b3
END  (* a b in order *) ;
```

```
BEGIN  (* program body *)
   writeln ('Type two three-letter words, one per line');
   readln (a1, a2, a3);   readln (b1, b2, b3);
   CASE abinorder OF
      true : writeln (a1,a2,a3, ' ', b1,b2,b3);
      false : writeln (b1,b2,b3, ' ', a1,a2,a3)
   END  (* CASE *)
END.
```

Figure 9.9

9.4 Exercises

*1.   (a) Modify your program for exercise 6.2.1 so that the rocket
drawing process becomes a procedure.
       (b) Incorporate a procedure which clears the terminal screen by
printing an appropriate number of blank lines. The program body is
to repeatedly obey your two procedures

      DrawRocket; ClearScreen

so that a new rocket appears at the bottom of the screen just as
the previous one disappears off the top.

*2. Modify your solution to exercise 3.3.9 to use a procedure which
works out and prints the change.

 3. Write a procedure to print the values of three integer variables in
ascending order and then rewrite your solution to exercise 4.5.14
incorporating this procedure.

 4. If your implementation permits program control of cursor movement,
write a program to move a rocket horizontally across the screen.
Use a procedure to draw a simple rocket

```
       *******
    ** ********
     **********
    ** ********
       *******
```

and one to move it one step to the right by 'extending' the nose

```
       ********
    ** *********
     ***********
    ** *********
       ********
```

and then 'reducing' the tail.

```
       *******
    ** ********
     **********
    ** ********
       *******
```

Your program should call the first procedure once and then call the second an appropriate number of times in a loop so that the rocket reaches the right hand edge of the screen.

*5. Modify your program for exercises 1, 2, 3 and 4 so that all entities are declared as locally as possible (if this is not already the case).

*6. Introduce procedures to any sizeable program you have written (eg the solution to exercise 7.6.13).

7. Define a function to convert a length, specified in yards, feet and inches, into inches and then modify your solution to exercise 2.7.5 to use this function.

*8. Define a function to compute n! and modify your solution to exercise 6.2.5 to incorporate this function.

9. Define a boolean function to determine whether three supplied letters are in alphabetical order and modify your solution to exercise 8.8.6 to use this function.

CHAPTER 10
Routine Information

The last chapter showed how to write routines (procedures and functions). If we want to carry out the same processing at two different points in a program, we can write one routine and call it twice.

This chapter extends this idea to show that we can use one routine to carry out two processes which are similar, but need not be exactly the same, or perhaps which are exactly the same but are applied to different values or variables. Every time we call the routine we give it some information to tell it what we want it to do during this particular call; and we supply the information in the form of <u>parameters</u>.

When we use a standard procedure (such as "read" and "write") or function (such as "sqrt", "odd" and "succ") we supply parameters to specify some information. In the case of "read" we specify the names of those <u>variables</u> to which the input values are to be assigned. For the others, we specify the <u>values</u> upon which the routine is to operate.

The standard procedures and functions are self-contained. All the information they require is supplied via parameters; they make no non-local references. Program transparency is greatly improved if routines are self-contained; the information a routine requires is made explicit. A further advantage is that a self-contained routine is easily portable; it can easily be incorporated within a different program. Another programmer requiring the routine can use it without knowing anything more than the number and order of the parameters. It is good policy that all routines should be self-contained and so we shall make ours self-contained.

When we are defining parameters for our own routines, we declare the parameters, between brackets, after the routine identifier. As the foregoing discussion implies, we distinguish between <u>value</u> parameters and <u>variable</u> parameters.

10.1 Value parameters

If the processing which a routine must perform depends upon some specified <u>value</u>, that value should be supplied as a parameter. Value parameter declarations have the same form as ordinary variable declarations except that the word VAR is omitted and a semi-colon appears only if further parameter declarations follow.

As a first example, recall the program of figure 4.3. If the digit naming process were to be written as a procedure, it would take one value parameter. The program of figure 4.3, incorporating this procedure, would have the form shown in figure 10.1.

The parameter "d" declared within the procedure heading is called a <u>formal</u> parameter. The parameter "digit" supplied when the procedure is called is an <u>actual</u> parameter. The actual parameter may be any expression of a type compatible with that of the formal parameter.

121

Usually the two types will be the same but, for example, the actual parameter may have type "integer" if the formal has type "real".

The formal parameter is effectively an initialized local variable. It is a variable local to the procedure but, when the procedure is called, it is given the value of the actual parameter. So, in the program of figure 10.1, if the readln-statement were to give "digit" the value 7 then, when the procedure "Name" is called with "digit" as the actual parameter, the local variable "d" comes into being with the current value 7. In this program the actual parameter and the formal parameter have different names. This is not necessary but aids clarity.

```
PROGRAM DigitNamer (input, output);

    (* Names a supplied digit *)

VAR
    digit : integer;

PROCEDURE Name (d : integer);
BEGIN
    write ('This is ');
    CASE d OF
        0 : writeln ('zero');
        1 : writeln ('one');
        2 : writeln ('two');
        3 : writeln ('three');
        4 : writeln ('four');
        5 : writeln ('five');
        6 : writeln ('six');
        7 : writeln ('seven');
        8 : writeln ('eight');
        9 : writeln ('nine')
    END (* CASE *)
END  (* Name *) ;

BEGIN  (* program body *)
    write ('Give me a digit ');   readln (digit);
    Name (digit)
END.
```

Figure 10.1

To name several different digits the procedure would be called with a different parameter each time. For example, recalling the program of figure 3.4, each digit of a three-digit integer n would be named by the three successive calls

```
Name (n DIV 100);
Name ((n MOD 100) DIV 10);
Name (n MOD 10)
```

As a second example consider the quadratic equation solver of figure 4.9. The solving process requires the three coefficients of the equation. Written as a procedure, it would have three value parameters, all of type "real". The procedure heading could have the form

        PROCEDURE QuadSolve (a : real; b : real; c : real);

but, as with ordinary declarations, adjacent declarations of the same type can be concatenated. The heading can be written

        PROCEDURE QuadSolve (a, b, c : real);

When the procedure is called, it must be supplied with three actual parameters and the order in which they are supplied is significant. Each formal parameter will correspond to the actual parameter which is in the same position in the parameter list.

All the other entities declared in figure 4.9 are local to the equation solving process and so should be declared within the procedure. A program equivalent to that of figure 4.9, but incorporating a procedure, is given in figure 10.2. In this case, the actual parameters have the same names as the formal parameters.

```
PROGRAM QuadEqn (input, output);

    (* Solves a quadratic equation *)

    VAR
       a, b, c : real;

    PROCEDURE QuadSolve (a, b, c : real);
       CONST
          assumedzero = 1E-9;
       VAR
          x1, x2, disc, rootofdisc, repart, impart : real;
    BEGIN
       disc := sqr(b) - 4*a*c;
       IF disc > assumedzero THEN

          . . .        { as in figure 4.9 }

             writeln (-b/(2*a) :6:2)
          END
    END   (* Quad solve *) ;

BEGIN   (* program body *)
    writeln ('Give the coefficients');
    readln (a, b, c);
    QuadSolve (a, b, c)
END.
```

                    Figure 10.2

Returning to our examination mark program of figure 9.4 we have three procedures which refer to the values of non-local variables. The body of the procedure "ListTopsAndFails" is as in figure 9.3 and uses the values of "noofstudents", "average" and "topmark". It should therefore be defined to take three value parameters. If we wish the procedure body to remain unchanged, the procedure heading will have the form

```
PROCEDURE ListTopsAndFails
    (noofstudents, topmark : integer;  average : real);
```

However, if we decide to change the names of the formal parameters, the heading might be

```
PROCEDURE ListTopsAndFails
    (nstuds, topm : integer;  avem : real);
```

and we would then have to replace "noofstudents" by "nstuds", "topmark" by "topm" and "average" by "avem" throughout the procedure body. In either case, assuming the three global variables retain their original names, the procedure call in the program body becomes

```
ListTopsAndFails (noofstudents, topmark, average)
```

The other non-local references to values in this program are the occurrences of "average", "topmark", "passmark" and "noofstuds" within the procedure "Headings". If we give this procedure four value parameters, it will have the form shown in figure 10.3 and the procedure call will be

```
Headings (average, topmark, passmark, noofstudents)
```

```
PROCEDURE Headings
      (ave : real;  topm, passm, nstuds : integer);
BEGIN
   rewrite (tops);  rewrite (fails);
   writeln (tops, 'Number of candidates: ', noofstudents :1);
   writeln (fails, 'Number of candidates: ', noofstudents :1);

   writeln (tops, 'Average mark: ', average :4:1);
   writeln (fails, 'Average mark: ', average :4:1);

   writeln (tops, 'Highest mark: ', topmark :1);
   writeln (tops);
   writeln (tops, 'Candidates with highest mark:');

   writeln (fails, 'Pass mark: ', passmark :1);
   writeln (fails);
   writeln (fails, 'Candidates below pass mark:')
END  (* Headings *) ;
```

Figure 10.3

All the functions defined in section 9.3 should take parameters. The function of figure 9.5 requires the number and the power:

FUNCTION powered (x : real; n : integer) : real;

The function of figure 9.6 needs to know the integer being tested:

FUNCTION prime (n : integer) : boolean;

The function of figure 9.7 should take the age as a parameter:

FUNCTION groupfor (age : integer) : char;

The function of figure 9.8 requires the bound:

FUNCTION minfibover (bound : integer) : integer;

The function of figure 9.9 needs six letters:

FUNCTION inorder (a1, a2, a3, b1, b2, b3 : char) : boolean;

These functions could then easily be applied to several different values. For example, suppose we wish to extend the powering program of figure 9.5 to read two real numbers x and y and two integers n and m and to compute the values

$$x^m \qquad y^n \qquad (x^n)^m \qquad (y^m)^n$$

Using the function "powered" we can compute these values as

powered (x, m)
powered (y, n)
powered (powered (x, n), m)
powered (powered (y, m), n)

The complete program is shown in figure 10.4.

Value parameters transfer information <u>into</u> a routine and so are sometimes called <u>input</u> <u>parameters</u>.

10.1.1 <u>Assignment to a value parameter</u>

We are allowed to change the value of a formal value parameter inside a procedure but this does not affect the actual parameter. The program of figure 10.5 illustrates this. The output from this program is

m has the value 27
     27   54   108   216
m now has the value 27

The same value is output by both writeln-statements in the program body. When the procedure is called, the current value of "m" is assigned to "n" but subsequent changes to "n" do not affect the value of "m". If "DoubleUp" were called several times, each call would generate a new "n" which would start life as a <u>copy</u> of "m".

```
PROGRAM Powers (input, output);

    (* Given x, y, m and n, the program forms

        x^m, y^n, (x^n)^m, (y^m)^n *)

VAR
  x, y : real;
  m, n : integer;

FUNCTION powered (x : real;  n : integer) : real;
  VAR
    i : integer;
    p, xsquared : real;
BEGIN
  IF n = 1 THEN powered := x ELSE
  BEGIN
    xsquared := sqr (x);
    IF odd (n) THEN p := x * xsquared ELSE
      p := xsquared;
    FOR i := 2 TO n DIV 2 DO
      p := p * xsquared;
    powered := p
  END
END  (* powered *);

BEGIN  (* program body *)
  writeln ('Give me two real numbers and two positive integers');
  readln (x, y, m, n);

  writeln (x, ' raised to the power ', m :2, ' =', powered (x,m));
  writeln (y, ' raised to the power ', n :2, ' =', powered (y,n));
  writeln (x, ' raised to the power ', n :2,
               ' all raised to the power ', m :2, ' =',
                         powered (powered (x,n), m));
  writeln (y, ' raised to the power ', m :2,
               ' all raised to the power ', n :2, ' =',
                         powered (powered (y, m), n))
END.
```

Figure 10.4

10.2 Variable parameters

If a routine is to change the value of a variable it must have access to
the variable, not just its value. To make the routine self-contained it
must take a variable parameter. To indicate that a list of formal
parameters (up to a semi-colon or right hand bracket) comprises variable
parameters, we precede the list by the reserved word VAR. As with value
parameters, a formal variable parameter is local to the procedure.

```
PROGRAM AssignToValueParameter (output);

    (* Illustrates the effect of
       assigning to a value parameter *)

VAR
    m : integer;

PROCEDURE DoubleUp (n : integer);
    VAR
        i : integer;
BEGIN
    write (n);
    FOR i := 1 TO 3 DO
    BEGIN
        n := n * 2;    write (n)
    END;
    writeln
END  (* Double up *);

BEGIN  (*program body*)
    m := 27;
    writeln ('m has the value ', m :1);

    DoubleUp (m);
    writeln ('m now has the value ', m :1)
END.
```

                        Figure 10.5

An <u>actual</u> parameter corresponding to a formal variable parameter
must be a <u>variable</u> and must have the same type as that of the formal
parameter. When the routine is obeyed, all references to the formal
parameter are interpreted as references to the actual parameter.
Consequently, if a procedure assigns a value <u>to</u> a formal variable
parameter <u>before</u> it wishes to use the value posessed <u>by</u> that parameter,
the actual parameter need have no defined value when it is supplied.

It was mentioned in section 9.3 that a function should cause <u>no</u>
non-local changes. Consequently a function should take <u>no</u> variable
parameters (but, for reasons of efficiency, we shall relax this
condition later). It is to be expected, however, that a procedure might
change the values of some non-local variables. To make these side
effects obvious, it is especially important that a procedure should
indicate which variables it may change.

Look again at the first program we wrote containing a procedure -
the program of figure 9.1. The procedure "StateWordLength" refers to the
value of a non-local variable "length" and so should be modified to take
a value parameter.

```
PROCEDURE State (length : integer);
BEGIN
    writeln ('Word contains ', length :1, ' characters')
END  (* State *) ;
```

The procedure "DetermineWordength" refers to the same non-local
variable but the first thing it does is to set it to zero. So, it does
not make use of any value the variable might already have; the purpose
of the procedure is to give the variable a value. This procedure is
going to change the value of a non-local variable so, to make the fact
explicit, we should supply the variable as a variable parameter. The
procedure call becomes

        Determine (length)

and the procedure could have the form shown in figure 10.6.

```
PROCEDURE Determine (VAR len : integer);
BEGIN
    len := 0;
    REPEAT
        len := len + 1;   get (input)
    UNTIL NOT (input^ IN ['a'..'z', '-', ''''])
END  (* Determine *) ;
```

                        Figure 10.6

We can improve upon this. Any processing inside a procedure which
is purely local to that procedure should be handled by local variables;
so, in this case, the variable that works out the length should be
local. In figure 10.6, "len" is a parameter of the procedure and, hence,
apparently local to the procedure; but, because "len" is a variable
parameter, references to "len" within the procedure body become
references to the (non-local) actual parameter when the procedure body
is obeyed. An improved version of the procedure is in figure 10.7.

```
PROCEDURE Determine (VAR size : integer);
    VAR
        len : integer;
BEGIN
    len := 0;
    REPEAT
        len := len + 1;   get (input)
    UNTIL NOT (input^ IN ['a'..'z', '-', '''']);
    size := len
END  (* Determine *) ;
```

                        Figure 10.7

The length is computed by "len", a local variable, and the final value is assigned to the variable parameter, "size".

In section 10.1 we ensured that all the procedures in our examination mark program were self-contained so far as references to values were concerned. We now turn our attention to non-local changes to variables.

The procedure "ComputeTopAndAverage" gives values to three non-local variables: "noofstudents", "topmark" and "average". It should therefore take three variable parameters. If the procedure body is to remain unchanged, its heading would be

```
PROCEDURE Compute
        (VAR noofstudents, topmark : integer;
         VAR average : real);
```

and its call would be

```
Compute (noofstudents, topmark, average)
```

Program transparency is greatly improved by the occurrence, in the procedure call, of the three variables which the procedure changes. Notice that the word VAR must appear twice in the formal parameter list because the first occurrence takes effect only up to the semi-colon following "integer".

This procedure still displays a side effect not implied by the parameter list: it changes the file buffer variable "markfile^" by reading from the text file "markfile". To make the procedure completely self-contained this file should be included as a variable parameter of type "text". If, within the procedure body, we were to replace "markfile" by "mfile", "noofstudents" by "nstuds", "topmark" by "topm" and "average" by "avem", the procedure heading might be

```
PROCEDURE Compute
        (VAR mfile : text;
         VAR nstuds, topm : integer;  VAR avem : real);
```

The only non-local variables affected by "ListTopsAndFails" are the file buffer variables "markfile^", "fails^" and "tops^". This procedure should therefore be supplied with three variable text parameters in addition to its three value parameters

```
PROCEDURE ListTopsAndFails
        (VAR mfile, failfile, topfile : text;
         nstuds, topm : integer;    avem : real);
```

The two procedures "CopyToTops" and "CopyToFails" (see figure 9.3) are similar: each copies a line from one text file to another. The only difference is that, where one writes to "tops", the other writes to "fails". This suggests that, if the files involved were parameters, we could replace both procedures by one.

```
PROCEDURE CopyLine (VAR here, there : text);
   VAR
      ch : char;
BEGIN
   REPEAT
      read (here, ch);    write (there, ch)
   UNTIL eoln (here);
   writeln (there)
END  (* Copy Line *) ;
```

Now, to achieve the effect of

```
CopyToTops
```

we write

```
CopyLine (markfile, tops)
```

and for

```
CopyToFails
```

we write

```
CopyLine (markfile, fails)
```

This use of files illustrates one of the main advantages of parameters: within one program, the same routine can be called with different sets of parameters.

Using the same technique, we can apply procedures to output information before and after each list of candidates. This is done by the program of figure 10.8. We have now completed our modifications to the examination mark program of figure 9.4: all the routines are self-contained.

```
PROGRAM ExamMarks (markfile, tops, fails);

    (* Processes a file of examination marks *)

   VAR
      markfile, tops, fails : text;
      noofstudents, topmark: integer;
      average : real;

   PROCEDURE Compute
        (VAR mfile : text;
         VAR nstuds, topm : integer;  VAR avem : real);
      VAR
         mark, total, stud : integer;
   BEGIN
      reset (mfile);   readln (mfile, nstuds);
      total := 0;   topm := 0;
```

```
        FOR stud := 1 TO nstuds DO
        BEGIN
           readln (mfile, mark);    total := total + mark;
           IF mark > topm THEN topm := mark
        END;
        avem := total / nstuds
END  (* Compute *) ;

PROCEDURE ListTopsAndFails
        (VAR mfile, failfile, topfile : text;
         nstuds, topm : integer;    avem : real);
     VAR
        mark, stud, topcount, failcount : integer;
        passmark : integer;

     PROCEDURE CopyLine (VAR here, there : text);
        VAR
           ch : char;
        BEGIN
          REPEAT
             read (here, ch);    write (there, ch)
          UNTIL eoln (here);
          writeln (there)
        END  (* Copy line *) ;

     PROCEDURE Footing (VAR f : text;  n : integer);
        BEGIN
           writeln (f);
           writeln (f, 'Number of candidates: ', n :1)
        END  (* Footing *) ;

     PROCEDURE Heading
           (VAR f : text;  n, top, pass : integer;  ave : real);
        BEGIN
           rewrite (f);
           writeln (f, 'Number of candidates: ', noofstudents :1);
           writeln (f, 'Average mark: ', average :4:1);
           writeln (f, 'Highest mark: ', topmark :1);
           writeln (f, 'Pass mark: ', passmark :1);
           writeln (f)
        END  (* Heading *) ;

BEGIN  (* List tops and fails *)
     passmark := trunc (2 * avem / 3);
     Heading (topfile, nstuds, topm, passmark, avem);
     Heading (failfile, nstuds, topm, passmark, avem);
     writeln (topfile, 'Candidates with highest mark:');
     writeln (failfile, 'Candidates below pass mark:');

     reset (mfile);    readln (mfile, nstuds);
     topcount := 0;    failcount := 0;
     FOR stud := 1 TO nstuds DO
     BEGIN
        read (mfile, mark);
        IF mark < passmark THEN
        BEGIN
```

```
                    failcount := failcount + 1;
                    CopyLine (mfile, failfile)
                END ELSE
                    IF mark = topm THEN
                    BEGIN
                        topcount := topcount + 1;
                        CopyLine (mfile, topfile)
                    END;
                readln (markfile)
            END;

            Footing (failfile, failcount);
            Footing (topfile, topcount)
        END   (* List tops and fails *) ;

    BEGIN (* program body *)
        Compute (markfile, noofstudents, topmark, average);
        ListTopsAndFails
                (markfile, fails, tops, noofstudents, topmark, average)
    END.
```

Figure 10.8

10.3 Formal routines

It is possible to make one routine a parameter of another. A procedure
to tabulate a function could be an example of this. We may wish to
tabulate different functions at different times, so it is convenient to
supply the function as a parameter to the procedure. The procedure
heading will therefore include a formal function. The procedure call
will contain the name of an actual function. The declaration of a formal
procedure or function takes the same form as a normal procedure or
function heading.

     The program of figure 10.9 tabulates

        sin (x)

at 10 points over the interval [-1,1] and the function

        sin (x) / (x+1)

at 20 points over the interval [0,2π].

```
PROGRAM FnTabulation (output);

    (* Tabulates the functions
       sin (x)  and  sin (x) / (x+1) *)

CONST
    pi = 3.14159;

FUNCTION sinxoverxplus1 (x : real) : real;
BEGIN
    sinxoverxplus1 := sin (x) / (x + 1)
END  (* sin x over x+1 *) ;

PROCEDURE Tabulate
        (FUNCTION f (x : real) : real;
         a, b : real;  npts : integer);
    VAR
        i : integer;
        x, step : real;
BEGIN
    step := (b-a) / (npts-1);
    FOR i := 1 TO npts DO
    BEGIN
        x := a + (i-1) * step;
        writeln (i :3, x :7:4, f(x))
    END
END  (* Tabulate *) ;

BEGIN  (* program body *)
    writeln ('sin (x)');   writeln;
    Tabulate (sin, -1, 1, 10);
    writeln;   writeln;

    writeln ('sin (x) / (x+1)');   writeln;
    Tabulate (sinxoverxplus1, 0, 2*pi, 20)
END.
```

                          Figure 10.9

10.4 Forward references

It was stated in section 10.1 that the declaration of a procedure must precede its calls. So, for example, the following program outline is illegal

```
PROGRAM p ( ... );

    PROCEDURE a (i : integer);
        VAR
            ch : char;
```

```
BEGIN
   ...;   b (ch, i);   ...
END (* a *);

PROCEDURE b (c : char;  VAR n : integer);
BEGIN
   ...
END (* b *);

BEGIN
   ...
END.
```

because the call of "b" (within the body of "a") precedes its declaration. However, we may have a reason for wishing to declare "a" before "b". For example, when several procedures are declared at the same block level it is useful to order their declarations alphabetically so that they can be easily located.

Accordingly, Pascal provides a relaxation of this rule. A routine heading must be declared before the routine is called but its body may be declared later (but at the same block level). The declaration of the heading takes the form of a forward reference. The routine heading is presented but its body is replaced by

```
forward;
```

When its body is declared later, it is preceded by an abbreviated heading. Only the routine identifier appears following either PROCEDURE or FUNCTION. No mention is made of any parameters, nor in the case of a function, the type of the function. The program outline above becomes

```
PROGRAM p ( ... );

   PROCEDURE b (c : char;  VAR n : integer);
      forward;

   PROCEDURE a (i : integer);
      VAR
         ch : char;
   BEGIN
      ...;   b (ch, i);   ...
   END (* a *);

   PROCEDURE b;
   BEGIN
      ...
   END (* b *);

BEGIN
   ...
END.
```

If the procedure "CopyLine" of figure 10.8 were used in this way, its forward reference would be

```
        PROCEDURE CopyLine (VAR here, there : text);
           forward;
```

and its actual declaration later would be

```
        PROCEDURE CopyLine;
           VAR
              ch : char;
        BEGIN
           ...        { as in figure 10.8 }
        END  (* Copy Line *);
```

If the function "powered" of figure 10.4 became a forward reference, its heading would be introduced in the form

```
        FUNCTION powered (x : real;  n : integer) : real;
           forward;
```

and its actual declaration later would be

```
        FUNCTION powered;
           VAR
              i : integer;
              p, xsquared : real;
        BEGIN
           ...        (* as in figure 10.4 *)
        END  (* powered *);
```

10.5 Exercises

*1. Modify your solutions to the exercises of chapter 9 so that all the routines are self-contained.

2.   (a) Define a boolean function which determines whether two real values agree within some specified tolerance.

(b) Define three boolean functions to check whether a triangle, specified by three lengths is equilateral (all three sides of equal length), isosceles (two sides equal) or scalene (no two sides equal). Two values are to be regarded as equal if they differ by less than some accepted tolerance.

(c) Define three boolean functions to check whether a triangle is acute (all angles less than 90 degrees), right-angled (one angle is of 90 degrees) or obtuse (one angle exceeds 90 degrees).

(d) Define a boolean function to check that three supplied lengths do constitute a triangle.

(e) Write a program incorporating these functions to classify a sequence of supposed triangles.

3. Define a function to compute the cube root of a supplied real value. The cube root of a value v can be computed by an algorithm similar to that described in exercise 7.6.3 but with x repeatedly replaced by

$$\frac{2x + v/x^2}{3}$$

*4.   (a) Define a function to produce the highest common factor of two positive integers using the algorithm suggested in exercise 7.6.5.
(b) Using this function, define a function to compute the highest common factor of three positive integers.

5. Write a procedure to print the Morse code of any supplied letter and incorporate this procedure within a program to translate a sentence into Morse code. Assume each word contains only letters, successive words are separated by at least one space or end of line and the last word of the sentence is followed by a full stop. The Morse code should be produced one word per line with adjacent letters separated by at least one space.

*6.   (a) Write a procedure to print a given character a specified number of times.

(b) Include this within a procedure to draw a triangle. One parameter specifies the height of the triangle, a second indicates the character of which the triangle is to be composed and a third stipulates the number of spaces that will precede the apex. Four successive calls with parameter sets

        (3, '*', 10) (5, '+', 10) (7, '-', 10) (2, 'a', 10)

should produce the following output

```
         *
        ***
       *****
         +
        +++
       +++++
      +++++++
     +++++++++
         -
        ---
       -----
      -------
     ---------
    -----------
   -------------
         @
        @@@
```

7.   (a) Write

        PROCEDURE Delay (n : integer);

which does nothing other than simply waste time. It is to obey a loop n times and do something trivial each time.
   (b) Incorporate this procedure within your program for exercise 9.4.4 to make your rocket accelerate as it crosses the screen. Do this by causing a delay between 'steps' of the rocket and successively reduce the delay.

8.   (a) Introduce procedures to your solutions to exercise 6.2.16. You should use four procedures: one to travel up, one down, one right and one left.
   (b) Using these four procedures, write a procedure to draw a rectangle of specified dimensions. Test this procedure within a program to draw a flat-roofed house with windows and a door.
   (c) Write procedures to draw diagonal lines and use these to produce a procedure to draw a triangle. Use this procedure to put a roof on your house.

9. Modify your solution to exercise 6.2.6 to utilise a procedure which computes the mean and standard deviation of a supplied sample. The procedure should accept n as a value parameter and should return the two computed values via variable parameters.

*10. Modify your solution to exercise 9.4.3 to include

        PROCEDURE Order (VAR n1, n2 : integer)

to compare the values of two integer variables and, if they are not in ascending order, interchange them. Using this procedure, the values of three integer variables "a", "b" and "c" can be 'sorted' into ascending order by the three successive procedure calls

        Order (a, b);   Order (b, c);   Order (a, b)

11. A complex number may be represented by two values: the   real   part
    and the imaginary part. Write three procedures to process a complex
    number:

            one to read it,
            one to print it, and
            one to form its conjugate,

    and three procedures to process a pair of complex numbers:

            one to form the sum,
            one to form the difference, and
            one to form the product.

    Incorporate these within a program to read four complex numbers a,
    b, c, d and print the values of ab+cd and ab-cd together with their
    conjugates.

12. Write

        PROCEDURE Random
            (VAR x : integer; n : integer; VAR r : integer);

    to assign to the variable parameter "r" a psuedo-random integer in
    the range 1 to "n". Adopting the notation of section 7.5, the
    constants "a", "b" and "c" should be local to the procedure and the
    value of "x" should be updated.
        Test your procedure by calling it within a loop something like
    the following

            readln (n, x);
            FOR i := 1 TO 200 DO
            BEGIN
                Random (x, n, r);   write (r);
                IF i MOD 5 = 0 THEN writeln
            END

    and then incorporate this procedure in all the programs in which
    you have used a random number generator.

CHAPTER 11
Give it a Name

The predefined data types allow us to process numbers (integers and reals), truth values ("true" and "false") and characters and we can handle text files (which contain values of these types). We often wish to represent other things. Examples might be directions of travel (north, south, east, west) or pieces in a chess game (pawn, knight, bishop, rook, queen, king). We often wish to group data items together: we might have a collection of details of an employee or a set of candidates in an election. We sometimes wish to define relationships within a collection of data: a family tree would be one example.

Accordingly, Pascal allows us to define our own data types. In subsequent chapters we shall see how data can be grouped in different ways; in this chapter we shall learn to define new types to represent scalars (single items).

There are two classes of user-defined scalar types: symbolic types and subrange types. Both play a major role in improving the compile-time security of a program, both contribute to program efficiency and symbolic types in particular make a significant contribution to program transparency.

If a type is used in only one place it may be referred to anonymously. If it is used in more than one place it should be named. The type of a formal routine parameter and of a function result must be named. A new type is named in a type definition which has the form

```
    i = t;

where   i is an identifier
and     t is a type
```

A series of type definitions may appear between the constant declarations (if there are any) and the variable declarations (if there are any), heralded by the reserved word

TYPE

Thus the order of declarations within any one block is

Constants, Types, Variables, Procedures and functions

You might find this ordering easier to remember if you memorise a catch phrase. In full Pascal we must also cater for statement labels and these must be declared before anything else; so any phrase you come up with must start with an "L". Here are some examples:

Lazy Cows Trot Very Poorly

Little Chillies Taste Very Pungent

Little Cats Tails Vary Profusely

Learners Come To Value Pascal

or, perhaps if you are a vegetarian,

Let's Cook Textured Vegetable Protein

To avoid confusion with other identifiers, we shall usually adopt the convention of using plurals for types.

11.1 Symbolic types

A symbolic type (often called an enumerated type) is denoted by a bracketed list of user-defined names. Here are some symbolic types.

(north, south, east, west)
(white, red, yellow, green, brown, blue, pink, black)
(pawn, knight, bishop, rook, queen, king)
(cat, dog, rabbit, hamster, budgie, goldfish, frog, python)
(small, medium, large)
(male, female)

Each name is a constant and each collection of names constitutes a new type.

We can declare variables of symbolic type and we can assign to a symbolic variable the value of any expression of the same type. For example, the variable

d : (north, south, east, west);

can appear in the following assignment statement

d := south

If these types were named they might appear as the following type definitions

directions = (north, south, east, west);
snookerballs =
  (white, red, yellow, green, brown, blue, pink, black);
chesspieces = (pawn, knight, bishop, rook, queen, king);
pets =
  (cat, dog, rabbit, hamster, budgie, goldfish, frog, python);
sizes = (small, medium, large);
sexes = (male, female);

and the variable "d" would be declared as

d : directions;

Apart from assignment, the only operators which can be applied to symbolic values are the relational operators (<, <=, =, <>, >=, >) and the set membership operator IN. The relational operators act upon the ordering implied by the declaration and both operands must have the same type. For the symbolic types defined above, each of the following expressions delivers "true"

                    north < south
                    yellow < blue
                    queen > rook
            frog IN [goldfish .. python]

and, if "d" has been assigned the value "east" so do

            d = east
            d > south

but the following expressions are illegal.

                    red < queen
                    dog = medium
            d IN [small, large]

    Symbolic types are ordinal types and so may be used for case-
statement selectors and for-loop control variables and the standard
functions "ord", "succ" and "pred" are applicable. The ordinal number of
a symbolic value is the position of the value within the list when its
type is declared. The first value has ordinal number 0, the second
ordinal number 1, and so on. So, for the types declared earlier

            ord (south) = 1
            ord (black) = 7
            ord (bishop) = 2
            ord (small) = 0

    Interpretation of "succ" and "pred" is obvious. The successor of a
symbolic value, if it exists, is the value that comes next in the list;
and the predecessor, if it exists, is the value that comes before.

    Suppose we are writing a program to control the movement of a pen
on a piece of paper and that movement is restricted to four directions
(which we can call north, south, east and west). Assuming we know the
current direction of the pen and we want to turn right, how can we find
its new direction? Well, the first thing to do is to rearrange the
symbolic values of the data type "directions" so that they are taken in
order round the compass. If we take them clockwise, we get the following
data type.

            directions = (north, east, south, west);

Now the section of program is easy to write. If the current direction is
"west", the new direction will be "north"; but, in each of the other
three cases, the new direction will be the successor of the current one.
The following program fragment implements the process of turning right.

            IF d = west THEN
               d := north
            ELSE
               d := succ (d)

    A similar approach could be applied to turn left. If the current
direction is "north", the new direction is "west"; but, in each of the
other three cases, the new direction is the predecessor of the current
one.

```
FUNCTION turned
      (turn : turns;   d : directions) : directions;
BEGIN
   CASE turn OF
      right :
         IF d = west THEN
            turned := north
         ELSE
            turned := succ (d);
      left :
         IF d = north THEN
            turned := west
         ELSE
            turned := pred (d)
   END (* CASE *)
END (* turned *) ;
```

Figure 11.1

The function of figure 11.1 delivers the new direction and can turn
either left or right. It assumes the existence of the two data types

```
turns = (left, right);
directions = (north, east, south, west);
```

For the predefined data type "char" there exists a function "chr"
which maps an ordinal number onto the corresponding character. For a
symbolic type no equivalent function exists but can easily be defined.
The function of figure 11.2, given an integer in the range 0 to 7,
produces the snooker ball with that ordinal number.

Symbolics can be neither written nor read directly from a text file
but procedures can be constructed to achieve this. A value of type
"sizes" as defined earlier is printed by the procedure of figure 11.3
and if, for input purposes, a size is represented by its initial letter
then the procedure of figure 11.4 reads a size. Of course it is
important that, when the procedure of figure 11.4 is called, the next
character of the input stream is one of the six expected. If it is not,
an execution error will result. In a practical situation this would be
undesirable so the case-statement of figure 11.4 might be preceded by a
while-loop of the following form.

```
WHILE NOT (input^ IN ['S','s', 'M','m', 'L', 'l']) DO
BEGIN
   readln;
   writeln ('Please type one of the six characters: S s M m L l')
END
```

If the value of a snooker ball were typed as input, it could be
converted by the mapping function defined earlier. This is illustrated
by the procedure of figure 11.5.

```
FUNCTION ballwithvalue (n : integer) : snookerballs;
   VAR
      i : integer;
      b : snookerballs;
BEGIN
   b := white;
   FOR i := 1 TO n DO
      b := succ (b);
   ballwithvalue := b
END  (* ball with value *) ;
```

Figure 11.2

```
PROCEDURE WriteSize (size : sizes);
BEGIN
   CASE size OF
     small  : write ('small');
     medium : write ('medium');
     large  : write ('large')
   END (* CASE *)
END  (* Write size *) ;
```

Figure 11.3

```
PROCEDURE ReadSize (VAR size : sizes);
BEGIN
   CASE input^ OF
     'S', 's' : size := small;
     'M', 'm' : size := medium;
     'L', 'l' : size := large
   END (* CASE *);
   get (input)
END  (* Read size *) ;
```

Figure 11.4

```
PROCEDURE ReadBall (VAR ball : snookerballs);
   VAR
      v : integer;
BEGIN
   read (v);   ball := ballwithvalue (v)
END  (* Read ball *) ;
```

Figure 11.5

11.1.1 State indicators

One important application of symbolic types is as state indicators, to identify states of interest within and upon completion of a computational process. In particular they can identify states of interest within, and upon exit from, a multi-exit loop.

Remember our prime detector? In its most sophisticated form it attempted division of a supplied integer, n, by odd numbers 3, 5, ... until it found a factor of n or reached the square root of n. The program embodied a non-deterministic looping process with two possible reasons for exit - a factor found or the root reached. Using booleans (figure 8.8) we named the outcomes of the tests made to detect these states; using symbolics we can name the states themselves.

```
PROGRAM PrimeWithSymbolics (input, output);

        (* Tests the primality of a supplied integer *)

    VAR
        d, n, rootofn : integer;
        state : (stilltrying, factorfound, rootreached);

BEGIN
    write ('Give me an integer ');   readln (n);

    IF n < 2 THEN writeln ('*** too small ***') ELSE

      IF n < 4 THEN writeln (n, ' is prime') ELSE

        IF odd (n) THEN
        BEGIN
            rootofn := round (sqrt (n));
            d := 3;

            state := stilltrying;
            REPEAT
              IF n MOD d = 0 THEN state := factorfound ELSE
                IF d >= rootofn THEN state := rootreached ELSE
                  d := d + 2
            UNTIL state <> stilltrying;

            CASE state OF
              factorfound : writeln (n, ' is composite');
              rootreached : writeln (n, ' is prime')
            END (* CASE *)
        END ELSE
            writeln (n, ' is composite')
    END.

            Figure 11.6
```

At any point within the loop "we" (if we imagine that "we" are the computer) are in one of three states:
- no factor found yet but still trying,
- factor found,
- root reached.

We replace the boolean variables by a symbolic variable which can identify these three states

        state : (stilltrying, factorfound, rootreached)

and, within the loop, replace the two boolean assignments by appropriate assignments to this variable. The assignment

            factorfound := n MOD d = 0

becomes

        IF n MOD d = 0 THEN state := factorfound

and

            rootreached := d >= rootofn

becomes

        IF d >= rootofn THEN state := rootreached

We make the two tests <u>before</u> we update "d" and update "d" only if the tests fail. We initialise "state" prior to loop entry

        state := stilltrying

and the loop termination test becomes

        state <> stilltrying

Upon exit from the loop, "state" must have one of the two values

        "factorfound"   and   "rootreached"

and we use a case-statement to distinguish them.

        CASE state OF
            factorfound : ...;
            rootreached : ...
        END (* CASE *)

The program is in figure 11.6.

We can use a symbolic type to record <u>all</u> the possible states rather than just those within the loop. This is illustrated in the program of figure 11.7. The set membership test has been included purely to show an application of sets.

```
PROGRAM PrimeWithSymbolics (input, output);

    (* Tests the primality of a supplied integer *)

    VAR
        d, n, rootofn : integer;
        nis : (toosmall, beingdivided, prime, composite);

    BEGIN
        write ('Give me an integer ');   readln (n);
```

```
      IF n < 2 THEN nis := toosmall ELSE

      IF n IN [2, 3, 5, 7, 11, 13, 17, 19, 23,
               29, 31, 37, 41, 43, 47, 53, 59, 61] THEN
        nis := prime
      ELSE
        IF odd (n) THEN
        BEGIN
           rootofn := round (sqrt (n));
           d := 3;
           nis := beingdivided;
           REPEAT
              IF n MOD d = 0 THEN nis := composite ELSE
                 IF d >= rootofn THEN nis := prime ELSE
                    d := d + 2
           UNTIL nis <> beingdivided
        END ELSE
           nis := composite;

   CASE nis OF
      toosmall  :  writeln (n, ' is too small');
      composite :  writeln (n, ' is composite');
      prime     :  writeln (n, ' is prime')
   END (* CASE *)
END.
```

Figure 11.7

The technique of using a symbolic variable to indicate the state as control flows round a loop, in conjunction with a case-statement to determine the state upon exit, is very important; so here is another example. The program of figure 11.8 compares two lines of text (one from file "f1" and one from file "f2") and prints one of four different messages. It contains a loop which has four reasons for exit, so it uses a five-state symbolic type.

```
   PROGRAM LineComparison (f1, f2, output);

      (* Compares two lines for four possible outcomes *)

   VAR
      f1, f2 : text;
      weare : (comparing, atamismatch,
               atendoffirst, atendofsecond, atendofboth);
   BEGIN
      reset (f1);   reset (f2);
      weare := comparing;
      REPEAT
         IF eoln (f1) AND eoln (f2) THEN
            weare := atendofboth ELSE
         IF eoln (f1) THEN weare := atendoffirst ELSE
```

```
              IF eoln (f2) THEN weare := atendofsecond ELSE
               IF f1^ <> f2^ THEN weare := atamismatch ELSE
               BEGIN
                 get (f1);   get (f2)
               END
     UNTIL weare <> comparing;

     CASE weare OF
       atendofboth :
         writeln ('The two lines are the same');
       atendoffirst :
         writeln ('Line from f1 is shorter');
       atendofsecond :
         writeln ('Line from f2 is shorter');
       atamismatch :
          writeln ('Mismatch encountered')
     END (* CASE *)
   END.
```

Figure 11.8

11.2 Subrange types

A variable of ordinal type (boolean, char, integer, symbolic) can be restricted to a subrange. The variable is then said to have a subrange type but inherits all the properties of its <u>host</u> type. Any attempt to give a subrange variable a value outside its permitted range constitutes an error. Notice that subranges of type "real" are not allowed.

A subrange type is denoted by the upper and lower bounds separated by two dots. These bounds must be constants and the ordinal number of the lower bound must not exceed the ordinal number of the upper bound. Here are some subrange types

```
        1 .. maxint
      -10 .. 10
       -1 .. 17
      'A' .. 'Z'
      '0' .. '9'
```

and, assuming the existence of the symbolic types introduced earlier, some more, this time named.

```
        colourballs = yellow .. black
        capturablepieces = pawn .. queen
        furrypets = cat .. hamster
        littlepets = hamster .. frog
```

Subrange types may be defined in terms of user-defined constants. For example, a program containing the declarations

```
        CONST
          firstvowel = 'a';   lastvowel = 'u';
          n = 27;
```

could utilise the subrange types

```
firstvowel .. lastvowel

    1 .. n
```

Subrange types allow us to check the sensible use of variables. From the problem domain we decide what range of values should be sensible for each variable and specify this range in the declaration of the variable. Any attempt to assign a value outside the expected range will be prevented. So, by using subranges, we are helping the computer to detect our mistakes. Minimal subranging should always be the aim. We now consider the subranges that should have been used in some previous examples.

"NextYearsAge" (figure 2.6)

An age cannot be negative and is unlikely to exceed, say, 120.

```
CONST
    maxage = 120;
VAR
    agenow : 0 .. maxage;
```

"NextYearsAgeWithPrompt" (figure 2.7)

See "NextYearsAge" (figure 2.6).

"BoxWithRead" (figure 2.8)

For any practical box, the length of each side must exceed 0.

```
VAR
    length, width, depth : 1 .. maxint;
```

"PetShop" (figure 2.9)

The number in stock of any one species cannot be negative and we can impose a reasonable upper limit, say, 1000.

```
CONST
    maxpets = 1000;
VAR
    pet0s, pet2s, pet3s, pet4s : 0 .. maxpets;
```

"Box" (figure 3.1)

If the length of each side exceeds 0, then the base area will also exceed 0.

```
VAR
    length, width, depth, basearea : 1 .. maxint;
```

"TomDickandHarry" (figure (3.2)

The number of votes cast in an election cannot be negative.

```
VAR
    tomsvotes, dicksvotes, harrysvotes : 0 .. maxint;
```

"ReverseInt" (figure 3.4)

A three-digit integer must have at least one hundred and can have no more than nine hundreds, tens or units.

```
        VAR
            hundreds : 1 .. 9;
            tens, units : 0 .. 9;
```

"DigitNamer" (figure 4.3)

A digit is an integer in the range 0 to 9.

```
        VAR
            digit : 0 .. 9;
```

"InsuranceGrouping" (figure 4.5)

The program assumes that the age is in the range 15 to 64.

```
        VAR
            age : 15 .. 64;
```

"ChronologicalDates" (figure 4.8)

A day must be in the range 1 to 31, a month must be in the range 1 to 12 and a year must be in a sensible range, say 1800 to 2000.

```
        CONST
            firstyear = 1800;    lastyear = 2000;
        VAR
            d1, d2 : 1 .. 31;
            m1, m2 : 1 .. 12;
            y1, y2 : firstyear .. lastyear;
```

"Reverse4LetterWord" (figure 5.1)

The characters typed are supposed to be letters. If we assume that they will all be upper case letters, we can replace the data type "char" by the subrange 'A'..'Z'; but if we assume they will all be lower case letters, we should use the subrange 'a'..'z'. If they may be either upper or lower case letters we have a problem. Do we use the subrange 'a'..'Z' or the subrange 'A'..'z'? Well, this is implementation dependent; it depends whether the lower case letters come before or after the upper case letters. Subject to our earlier assumption that the lower case letters come after the upper case letters, we would use the subrange 'A'..'z' and we should include a comment to stress that this assumption has been made.

```
        (* Assumes that the upper case letters
           precede the lower case letters *)
        VAR
            c1, c2, c3, c4 : 'A' .. 'z';
```

Of course, this does not necessarily restrict the values of these variables to letters. Other characters may occur between the two groups of characters and some control characters may occur within each group.

"GiveName" (figure 5.2)

The program assumes that the initial will be A, B, C or F so the minimal subrange is A to F.

```
        VAR
            initial : 'A' .. 'F';
```

"ThreeLetterWordsInOrder (figure 5.3)

    See "Reverse4LetterWord" (figure 5.1).

"PairPrice" (figure 5.7)

    The input number of cents must be in the range 0 to 99; so the doubled number of cents must lie in the range 0 to 198.

```
VAR
    cents : 0 .. 198;
```

"CharSet" (figure 6.1)

    The for-loop control variable cannot go outside the range 0 to the number of characters.

```
VAR
    i : 0 .. noofchars;
```

"Alphabets" (figure 6.3)

    The for-loop control variable works through all the lower case letters.

```
VAR
    l : 'a' .. 'z';
```

"RaiseToKnownPower" (figures 6.4 and 6.5)

    The programs assume that the power is not negative and the for-loop control variable cannot take a value less than 1.

```
VAR
    n : 0 .. maxint;
    power : 1 .. maxint;
```

"LoanRepay" (figure 6.6)

    The for-loop control variable cannot take a value outside the range 1 to the number of years.

```
VAR
    year : 1 .. noofyears;
```

"ExamMarks" (figure 6.8)

```
CONST
    maxstudents = 250;    maxmark = 100;
VAR
    stud, noofstudents : 1 .. maxstudents;
    topcount, failcount : 0 .. maxstudents;
    mark, topmark, passmark : 0 .. maxmark;
    total : 0 .. maxint;
    chcount : 1 .. namelength;
```

"DrawHistogram" (figure 6.11)

```
CONST
    linelength = 120;
VAR
    interval : 1 .. noofintervals;
    frequency : 0 .. linelength;
```

```
                 chcount : 1 .. linelength;
"MinFib" (figure 7.6)

         VAR
             bound, thisterm : 1 .. maxint;
             prevterm, termbeforethat : 0 .. maxint;

"DieTrials" (figure 7.9)

         CONST
             a = 29;   b = 7;   c = 1024;   cminus1 = 1023;
             nooftrials = 100;
             faces = 6;   minface = 1;   maxface = 6;
         VAR
             x : 0 .. cminus1;
             try : 1 .. nooftrials;
             prev, thrown : minface .. maxface;
             noofthrows : 0 .. maxint;

"LineLength" (figure 8.5)

         VAR
             chcount : 0 .. maxint;

"FileLength" (figure 8.6)

         VAR
             linecount : 0 .. maxint;

"InsuranceGroupWithFn" (figure 9.7)

         TYPE
             groups = 'A' .. 'D';
         VAR
             age : 15 .. 64;

         FUNCTION groupforage : groups;

"MinFibWithFn" (figure 9.8)

         TYPE
             fibnos = 2 .. maxint;
         VAR
             bound : 1 .. maxint;

         FUNCTION minfiboverbound : fibnos;
```

"DigitNamer" (figure 10.1)

    As with figure 4.3 we should use the subrange 0..9 but, because it
is now used to specify the type of a formal parameter, it must be a
named type.

```
         TYPE
             digits = 0 .. 9;
         VAR
             digit : digits;

         PROCEDURE Name (d : digits);
```

"prime" (section 10.1)

The prime detection programs all assume that n is greater than 1
and so we should use a suitable named subrange type.

            TYPE
                over1 = 2 .. maxint;

            FUNCTION prime (n : over1) : boolean;

Subrange types should be used within the function - the smallest divisor
tried is 3 and the root of n must be over 1.

            TYPE
                over1 = 2 .. maxint;

            FUNCTION prime (n : over1) : boolean;
                VAR
                    d : 3 .. maxint;
                    rootofn : over1;

"Powers" (figure 10.4)

Within the function "powered", the parameter "n" cannot be negative
and so should be constrained to the natural numbers.

            TYPE
                naturals = 0 .. maxint;
            VAR
                m, n : naturals;

            FUNCTION powered (x : real; n : naturals) : real;

"ballwithvalue" (figure 11.2)

The parameter must be an integer in the range 0 to 7.

            TYPE
                snookervalues = 0 .. 7;

            FUNCTION ballwithvalue (n : snookervalues) : snookerballs;

"ReadBall" (figure 11.5)

The integer read must be in the range 0 .. 7.

            VAR
                v : snookervalues;

11.2.1 Data entry validation

Subrange types provide a valuable protection against programming errors
and can also be used to detect data entry errors. For example, it was
mentioned that, in figure 4.3, the data type "integer" could be replaced
by the subrange type 0..9 and the program will accept no data value
outside this subrange. If a value outside the range is supplied, an
execution error results.

As was mentioned in section 11.1, programs which 'crash' when given
bad input are not to be encouraged so, for input data validation, it is
often better to use full range types to read values and then assign

these values to subrange variables only when it it is known that the values are in range. For example, to read a digit, we could use two variables

```
VAR
        d : 0 .. 9;
    dtyped : integer;
```

and then read values until one is in range.

```
REPEAT
  write ('Please type a digit ');    readln (dtyped)
UNTIL dtyped IN [0 .. 9];
d := dtyped
```

Of course, even this is not completely safe because an execution error will result if anything other than an integer is typed.

11.3 Exercises

*1. Define a named symbolic type to represent
        (i) days of the week,
       (ii) colours of the rainbow,
      (iii) eight points of the compass.

*2. Assuming the existence of your data type "days" as defined for exercise 1(i) define the following functions.

        (i) FUNCTION tomorrow (d : days) : days;
                to produce the day after the given day,

       (ii) FUNCTION yesterday (d : days) : days;
                to produce the day before the given day,

      (iii) FUNCTION lapsed (n : integer; d : days) : days;
                to produce the day which is n days from the given day.
                Assume that n may be positive or negative and
                incorporate your two functions of parts (i) and (ii).

*3. Introduce a symbolic type to represent states of interest within any program you have written containing a multi-exit loop (eg exercises 8.8.10 and 8.8.12).

*4. Write a program to 'merge' two ordered sequences of integers to produce one ordered sequence. The two supplied sequences are stored in text files, one integer per line, and the merged sequence is to be produced in a third file. Use a symbolic type to denote states of interest within the merging process.

 5. A carpet manufacturer controls his looms by computer. He supplies the computer with a series of colour codes indicating the order in which different colours are to be fed to the looms. Light shades used are yellow, cream, pink and orange; dark shades used are red, blue and green; and the code used for each colour is its initial letter. All his patterns are such that colours used must be alternately light and dark. Write a program to check that a series of colour codes, terminated by "z", does satisfy this condition.

6. Write a

    PROCEDURE ReadInt
        (VAR f : text; VAR n : integer; VAR outcome : outcomes);

    to read an integer from a text file "f". Before attempting to read
    a value, the procedure is to check that a non-space character
    occurs before the end of the file is reached and that this
    character is a digit, a plus sign or a minus sign. If it is a sign,
    the procedure is to check that the following character is a digit.
    The parameter "outcome" is to indicate the outcome of the attempt
    and the parameter "n" is to acquire the value supplied only if the
    attempt is successful. The data type "outcomes" is a symbolic type.

        outcomes = (success, eofreached, nonnumchar);

    Write a program which uses this procedure to read a series of
    numbers from a text file, given that several numbers may occur on
    one line.

*7. Rearranging the order of names within your definitions for exercise
    1 if necessary, define named subrange types to embrace only
        (i) the mid-week days,
        (ii) the northerly directions,
        (iii) the southerly directions.

8. Define four data types

        "years", "months", "days" and "periods"

    to represent a span of years, names of months, the number of days
    in a month and the number of days in a period which does not exceed
    one year. Then write

    FUNCTION daysbetween
        (y : years; d1 : days; m1 : months;
         d2 : days; m2 : months) : periods;

    to compute the number of days between day d1 of month m1 in year y
    and the next occurrence of day d2 of month m2. Test your function
    by incorporating it within a program.

*9. Introduce subrange types to some of your existing programs.

CHAPTER 12
Putting the Bits Together

Little has been said so far about the process of writing a program. Most programs have been presented as a fait accompli. In this chapter we examine the construction process and follow two examples through from initial outline to final program.

12.1 Top-down design

When we read a program we don't start at the first line and work our way steadily to the end. We start with the program body and then examine procedures in some order, referring to the declarations as appropriate. We write a program the same way. We start with the top level of program logic, the program body, and then develop the lower levels in simple steps. This is called top-down design and each step in the development is called a refinement of the program.

We define one level of program logic by giving names to the activities involved. To refine this we replace the named activities either by groups of statements (or further named activities) to perform the tasks or by procedure or function calls and decide what parameters, if any, are needed. Refinements are then applied to expand any named activities at these new levels and the process continues until the entire final program is produced. We adopted this approach with the program of figure 9.1 to compute the length of a word.

12.2 top-down Testing

Unless a program is short (and this is a relative term; a program considered short by the expert may seem very long to the novice), we do not write the whole program before running it. Instead we execute the program at various stages of its development in the hope that any mistakes we make might be spotted as we proceed. Thus our top-down design process incorporates top-down testing.

If an error comes to light it is probably caused by the changes we have made since the previous run. This knowledge considerably speeds up the process of locating and correcting errors. It is easier (and quicker in the long run) to run ten programs, each an extension of the previous one but each containing a (different) error, than to try sorting out all ten errors from one program (especially when more errors have crept in because of our ignorance of the errors we made early in the design process). This is particularly true of large programs containing thousands of lines.

Top-down design aims at getting the control structure of the program right. Locating and correcting simple errors such as forgetting to initialize a variable prior to entry to a loop or writing n := n+1 instead of n := n-1 is relatively straightforward. Errors in the control structure are far more troublesome. The control structure would be wrong if, for example, the test after an IF or WHILE were incorrect or, worse, an if-statement appears where a while-statement should be. Top-down testing aims at checking the control structure at regular intervals.

Always design a program with its full specification in mind, but test the overall structure on a simplified problem as soon as possible. Thereafter apply no more refinements between successive runs than you feel you can implement without error. As you improve, the number of error-free refinements you can introduce will increase. Good luck!

12.3 Dummy routines

During the construction of a program we often introduce a routine to indicate its role in the overall structure but wish to run the program before considering the routine body. A program to read an integer and perform different processing according as the integer is positive, negative or zero might have the following structure.

```
read (n);
IF n > 0 THEN ProcessPositive (n) ELSE
    IF n < 0 THEN ProcessNegative (n) ELSE
        ProcessZero
```

We may wish to implement "ProcessZero" and test the program before we define "ProcessPositive" and "ProcessNegative". We must supply declarations of these two other procedures or the program will not compile. We therefore supply them as dummy procedures. If we ensure that "n" acquires the value 0 these two dummy procedures will not be called so their bodies are of no significance. Consequently we can give them empty bodies. A compound statement may contain zero statements (ie one empty statement) so we can define our two dummy procedures as follows

```
PROCEDURE ProcessPositive (n : posints);
BEGIN
END  (* Process positive *) ;

PROCEDURE ProcessNegative (n : negints);
BEGIN
END  (* Process negative *) ;
```

where

```
posints = 1 .. maxint;
negints = -maxint .. -1;
```

and, when the program compiles, it can be run.

Your compiler should object if you supply an empty body for a function because the body must contain an assignment to the function identifier. We can produce a dummy function by assigning any value of the appropriate type. Here is an example.

```
FUNCTION fun (...) : integer;
BEGIN
   fun := 0
END  (* fun *) ;
```

If an empty procedure is called it has no apparent effect; when control reaches the empty body it immediately returns to the point of call. However it would be nice to know that the routine had been called. In the above example we may wish to define all the procedures as dummy routines and run the program three times, supplying a different value of "n" each time, to test the decision logic of the program body. On the other hand, if we expected to test "ProcessZero" but "ProcessZero" was not called it would be benificial to know which, if either, of the other two routines had been activated. It is conventional, therefore, for a dummy routine to write its name.

```
PROCEDURE ProcessPositive (n : posints);
BEGIN
   writeln ('Process positive')
END  (* Process positive *) ;

PROCEDURE ProcessNegative (n : negints);
BEGIN
   writeln ('Process negative')
END  (* Process negative *) ;
```

12.4 Case study 1

We are going to write a program to tidy up a chapter of text so that it can be printed neatly in pages of a specified length and width. We shall not align the right margin but we shall terminate a line at the earliest convenient point once the specified right hand margin has been reached. Paragraphs are to be separated and indented, sentences are to be separated by two spaces, words are to be separated by one space but no space is to separate a word from any punctuation character that follows it. We shall assume that words can contain hyphens and apostrophes and that the only other characters present in the text will be commas, colons, semicolons, question marks, exclamation marks and full stops.

We shall start the chapter with a new paragraph and use some special character to indicate where one paragraph ends and a new one starts; and we shall use some other character to mark the end of the whole chapter. If we use a star as the paragraph separator and a dollar to mark the end of the chapter we could have an input file like this:

```
Is    this      text
     tidy     ?No         ,it's      a
mess       !*     Right         ;    what
   can    we do about
it?We'll     write          a
       program      to         print
   it neatly      .*What     a
          good      idea  !   $
```

If we specify a page width of 20 and a page length of 7 or greater, the output file is to look like this:

```
     Is this text tidy?
No, it's a mess!
     Right; what can
we do about it?  We'll
```

```
            write a program to print
            it neatly.
                What a good idea!
```

You are advised to implement this program yourself as we work
through the design. We start at the top level of program logic – with a
procedure to tidy a chapter. To make it self-contained, we'll tell it
the name of the file that contains the rough text and the name of the
file that is to contain the neat version; we'll tell it the two special
characters we are using as the paragraph separator and the chapter
terminator; and we'll specify the position of the right hand margin and
the number of lines that are to constitute one page. Ignoring the body
of the procedure for the moment, the program has the form shown in
figure 12.1.

```
      PROGRAM TidyText (rough, neat);

         CONST
            maxwidth = 120;    maxlength = maxint;

         TYPE
            widths = 1 .. maxwidth;
            lengths = 1 .. maxlength;

         VAR
            rough, neat : text;

         PROCEDURE Chapter
               (VAR inf, outf : text;
                parasep, chapterm : char;
                margin : widths;    bottom : lengths);
         BEGIN
            . . .
         END (* Chapter *) ;

      BEGIN (* program body *)
         Chapter (rough, neat, '*', '$', 20, 34)
      END.
```

                        Figure 12.1

The maximum number of characters that can be printed on a line is
unlikely to be more than 120; but it is possible that the program might
be used to produce output with no pagination and so the maximum page
length is taken to be "maxint".

Now we consider the body of the procedure. The procedure must
repeatedly process paragraphs until it reaches the end of the chapter
and must skip any spaces which occur before the first paragraph or
between successive paragraphs. In order to recognise the chapter
terminator, it must also skip any spaces that follow the last paragraph.
The procedure body therefore has the following form

```
BEGIN (* Chapter *)
    reset (inf);   rewrite (outf);
    SkipSpaces;
    REPEAT
        Paragraph;   SkipSpaces
    UNTIL at end of chapter
END (* Chapter *) ;
```

and requires two further procedures. The procedure to process a paragraph will have the following basic form.

```
PROCEDURE Paragraph;
BEGIN
    REPEAT
        Sentence;   SkipSpaces
    UNTIL at end of paragraph
END (* Paragraph *) ;
```

It must skip any spaces between successive sentences of the paragraph and, in order to recognise the end of the paragraph, it has to skip any spaces after the last sentence of the paragraph; but it need not skip spaces before the first sentence of the paragraph because these will already have been skipped by a call of "SkipSpaces" within the body of the procedure "Chapter". We can now consider the procedure to process a sentence

```
PROCEDURE Sentence;
BEGIN
    REPEAT
        Word;   SkipSpaces
    UNTIL at end of sentence
END (* Sentence *) ;
```

and the procedure to process a word.

```
PROCEDURE Word;
BEGIN
    REPEAT
        CopyChar
    UNTIL at end of word
END (* Word *) ;
```

To process a word, we simply copy all the characters of the word from "inf" to "outf".

```
PROCEDURE CopyChar;
    VAR
        ch : char;
BEGIN
    read (inf, ch);   write (outf, ch)
END (* Copy char *) ;
```

We can do this copying without using a character variable. The form

```
PROCEDURE CopyChar;
BEGIN
    write (outf, inf^);   get (inf)
END (* Copy char *) ;
```

is equivalent to the one above.

Now that we know how we are going to copy a character, we can return to the procedure "Word" and implement the test for the end of the word

NOT (inf^ IN ['A'..'Z', 'a'..'z', '-', ''''])

and then consider our test for the end of a sentence. This test follows a call of "SkipSpaces" so we first consider that. There may be no spaces to skip so this procedure uses a while-loop.

```
PROCEDURE SkipSpaces;
BEGIN
   WHILE inf^ = ' ' DO
      get (inf)
END (* Skip spaces *) ;
```

Now that the process of skipping spaces has been defined, we can implement our test for the end of a sentence

inf^ IN ['.', '!', '?']

and for the end of a paragraph. The first thought is probably to recognise the end of a paragraph with the test

inf^ = parasep

and then terminate the procedure "Paragraph" with

get (inf)

to skip the paragraph separator once it has been recognised. However, this will not work for the last paragraph because the last paragraph is followed by the chapter terminator, not a paragraph separator. To recognise the end of this paragraph also, the test must be extended to

inf^ IN [parasep, chapterm]

and the chapter terminator must not be skipped (because then the procedure seeking the end of the chapter would not find it). Consequently, the procedure to process a paragraph has the following form

```
PROCEDURE Paragraph;
BEGIN
   REPEAT
      Sentence;   SkipSpaces
   UNTIL inf^ IN [parasep, chapterm];
   IF inf^ = parasep THEN
      get (inf)
END (* Paragraph *) ;
```

Now the test for the end of the chapter is straightforward:

inf^ = chapterm

We now have a complete Pascal program with a basic form suitable for expansion to the final version we require. But, before fully refining the program, it is useful to know that the basic structure generated so far is sensible. Although it caters for no internal punctuation other than hyphens and apostrophes and gives no consideration to line layout, it should recognise the end of each word, the end of each sentence, the end of each paragraph and the end of the

chapter; and the output file should contain everything in the input file
except the spaces and the special markers.

So we should run the program to verify that this is so. To do that,
we have to make a few changes. All the output will appear on one line
and this is obviously impractical so, to get some sensible output, we
can modify "SkipSpaces" so that it retains the end-of-line characters in
the original file. To confirm that the program recognises the start and
end of a word, we can enclose each word between two suitable characters
(say brackets). To confirm that the program recognises the end of a
sentence we can make it put some special character (say '/') at the end
of a sentence and we can make it start each new sentence on a new line.
To see when it is starting a new paragraph, we can make it precede the
first sentence of each paragraph by some special characters (say, three
plus signs).

With these modifications, the program is as in figure 12.2. If this
program is applied to the original data file (but with the comma and
semicolon removed) it produces the following output {Run number 1}.

```
+++(Is)(this)(text)
(tidy)?/
(No)(it's)(a)
(mess)!/
+++(Right)(what)
(can)(we)(do)(about)
(it)?/
(We'll)(write)(a)
(program)(to)(print)
(it)(neatly)./
+++(What)(a)
(good)(idea)!/
```

```
PROGRAM TidyTextRun1 (rough, neat);

    (* Delimits words within a chapter of text *)

  CONST
    maxwidth = 120;    maxlength = maxint;

  TYPE
    widths = 1 .. maxwidth;
    lengths = 1 .. maxlength;

  VAR
    rough, neat : text;

  PROCEDURE Chapter
      (VAR inf, outf : text;    parasep, chapterm : char;
       margin : widths;    bottom : lengths);

    PROCEDURE SkipSpaces;
    BEGIN
      WHILE inf^ = ' ' DO
        IF eoln (inf) THEN
```

```
            BEGIN
              readln (inf);   writeln (outf)
            END ELSE
              get (inf)
        END (* Skip spaces *);

    PROCEDURE Paragraph;

      PROCEDURE CopyChar;
      BEGIN
        write (outf, inf^);   get (inf)
      END (* Copy char *);

      PROCEDURE Sentence;

        PROCEDURE Word;
        BEGIN
          write (outf, '(');
          REPEAT
            CopyChar
          UNTIL NOT (inf^ IN ['A'..'Z', 'a'..'z', '-', '''']);
          write (outf, ')')
        END (* Word *);

      BEGIN (* Sentence *)
        REPEAT
          Word;   SkipSpaces
        UNTIL inf^ IN ['.', '!', '?'];
        CopyChar;   writeln (outf, '/')
      END (* Sentence *);

    BEGIN (* Paragraph *)
      write (outf, '+++');
      REPEAT
        Sentence;   SkipSpaces
      UNTIL inf^ IN [parasep, chapterm];
      IF inf^ = parasep THEN
        get (inf)
    END (* Paragraph *);

  BEGIN (* Chapter *)
    reset (inf);   rewrite (outf);
    SkipSpaces;
    REPEAT
      Paragraph;   SkipSpaces
    UNTIL inf^ = chapterm;
    get (inf)
  END (* Chapter *);

BEGIN
  Chapter (rough, neat, '*', '$', 20, 34)
END.
```

Figure 12.2

Now we can give thought to some of the missing details. We do not include them all at once. We extend the program slightly and then check the modifications we have just made. That way we have a good chance of spotting any mistakes as soon as we make them.

First, we'll consider the punctuation. Punctuation characters appear between successive words of a sentence so the sensible thing is to make the program do something about them between successive calls of "Word" within the procedure "Sentence". When the program has processed a word and skipped any spaces that follow it, it must check for a punctuation character. So we change the body of the loop within procedure "Sentence" from

        Word;   SkipSpaces

to

        Word;   SkipSpaces;   Punctuation

and define the following procedure.

```
PROCEDURE Punctuation;
BEGIN
   IF inf^ IN [',', ':', ';'] THEN
   BEGIN
      CopyChar;    SkipSpaces
   END
END (* Punctuation *) ;
```

With this modification, the program transforms the original input file to the following form {Run number 2}.

```
+++(Is)(this)(text)
(tidy)?/
(No),(it's)(a)
(mess)!/
+++(Right);(what)
(can)(we)(do)(about)
(it)?/
(We'll)(write)(a)
(program)(to)(print)
(it)(neatly)./
+++(What)(a)
(good)(idea)!/
```

Now we turn to the spacing, starting with the spacing between paragraphs. It is convenient to think of this spacing as being between successive paragraphs rather than as part of the paragraphs themselves. So, rather than produce the spacing with the procedure that processes a paragraph, we modify the section of program that calls it (the body of "Chapter").

We want all paragraphs indented (say five spaces) so all we need do is precede each call of "Paragraph" by

        write (outf, '   ')

and follow each call by

        writeln (outf)

but, instead, we shall use two procedures. When we come to consider the
line length and page length later, we shall have to keep a count of
characters and lines and update these counts every time "write" or
"writeln" is called so this will be easier if we use procedures which do
the counting as well as produce the output. For the moment, these
procedures will simply produce output; one will print a specified number
of spaces and one will move to a new line. The body of "Chapter" will
take the following form.

```
BEGIN (* Chapter *)
   reset (inf);   rewrite (outf);   SkipSpaces;
   REPEAT
      Space (5);   Paragraph;   NewLine;   SkipSpaces
   UNTIL inf^ = chapterm;
   get (inf)
END (* Chapter *) ;
```

The procedure "Space" will need a named type for its parameter. This
will be the integer subrange 1 to the maximum gap size required (5 in
this example).

```
CONST
   maxgap = 5;

TYPE
   gaps = 1 .. maxgap;

PROCEDURE Space (n : gaps);
BEGIN
   write (outf, ' ' :n)
END (* Space *) ;
```

The procedure "NewLine" simply calls "writeln":

```
PROCEDURE NewLine;
BEGIN
   writeln (outf)
END (* New Line *) ;
```

   If we now remove the statement that printed plus signs, and apply
our program to the original data file {Run number 3}, we get the
following output.

```
      (Is)(this)(text)
(tidy)?/
(No),(it's)(a)
(mess)!/
      (Right);(what)
(can)(we)(do)(about)
(it)?/
(We'll)(write)(a)
(program)(to)(print)
(it)(neatly)./
      (What)(a)
(good)(idea)!/
```

   To tackle the spaces between sentences, we turn to the call of
"Sentence" within the body of "Paragraph". We want two spaces before
every sentence but the first so we process the first sentence outside
the loop and call

          Space (2)

before any remaining sentences of the paragraph. There may be no further
sentences in the paragraph so the loop becomes a while-loop.

```
          BEGIN (* Paragraph *)
             Sentence;   SkipSpaces;
             WHILE NOT (inf^ IN [parasep, chapterm]) DO
             BEGIN
                Space (2);   Sentence;   SkipSpaces
             END;
             IF inf^ = parasep THEN
                get (inf)
          END (* Paragraph *) ;
```

If we now remove the temporary writeln-statement from the procedure
"Sentence" and apply the program to the original data file {Run number
4}, we get the following output.

```
          (Is)(this)(text)
      (tidy)?  (No),(it's)(a)
      (mess)!
          (Right);(what)
      (can)(we)(do)(about)
      (it)?  (We'll)(write)(a)
      (program)(to)(print)
      (it)(neatly).
          (What)(a)
      (good)(idea)!
```

   To achieve the correct spacing between words of a sentence, we turn
to the body of the procedure "Sentence". We do the same sort of thing
that we did for sentences within a paragraph; process the first outside
the loop and precede each one processed within the loop by the
appropriate number of spaces (in this case, one).

```
          BEGIN (* Sentence *)
             Word;  SkipSpaces;   Punctuation;
             WHILE NOT (inf^ IN ['.', '!', '?']) DO
             BEGIN
                Space (1);   Word;   SkipSpaces;   Punctuation
             END;
             CopyChar
          END (* Sentence *) ;
```

   If we remove the two statements that print brackets around a word
and apply the program to the original data file {Run number 5}, this is
the output we get:

```
            Is this text
      tidy? No, it's a
      mess!
            Right; what
      can we do about
      it? We'll write a
      program to print
      it neatly.
            What a
      good idea!
```

The text is now being printed reasonably neatly but still retains all the line boundaries that were present in the original data file and contains no pagination. To control line length and page length we need to count lines and characters on a line. To do this, we shall need two integer subrange variables (say "line" and "charsonline") declared local to "Chapter"

```
      VAR
         line : lengths;
         charsonline : 0 .. maxwidth;
```

and initialized

```
      line := 1;    charsonline := 0;
```

in the body of "Chapter".

The values of these variables must be subject to possible change (explicitly or implicitly) by all procedures local to "Chapter" with the exception of "SkipSpaces" and so should, perhaps, be passed to each of these procedures as a variable parameter. However, since they can be affected by almost <u>all</u> these procedures, there is some argument for including a comment to this effect and allowing each of these procedures to refer to the variables directly (ie non-locally rather than as a variable parameter).

The line indicator must be incremented and the character count reset to 0 inside "NewLine" and the character count must be incremented within "CopyChar" and "Space".

Each time the output reaches the bottom of a 'page', we must reinitialize the line counter and insert some suitable end-of-page marker in the output file. There is a Pascal procedure "page" available and the call

```
      page (outf)
```

will do this. However, as mentioned in chapter 5, the page marker may have no effect when the file is printed at a terminal; it may be necessary to write a few blank lines to the file instead.

Our aim is to terminate a line at the first convenient point once the designated right hand margin has been reached. So the procedure "SkipSpaces" should not terminate an output line; instead, the procedure "Space" is modified so that it calls "NewLine" rather than print any spaces if the spacing would take the number of characters on the line up to or beyond the right hand margin.

```
PROGRAM TidyText (rough, neat);

    (* Controls layout within a chapter of text *)
  CONST
    maxwidth = 120;    maxlength = maxint;

  TYPE
    widths = 1 .. maxwidth;
    lengths = 1 .. maxlength;

  VAR
    rough, neat : text;

  PROCEDURE Chapter
    (VAR inf, outf : text;
     parasep, chapterm : char;
     margin : widths;    bottom : lengths);

       (* The parameters of this procedure are
          referenced globally by the inner procedures *)
    CONST
      maxgap = 5;

    TYPE
      gaps = 1 .. maxgap;

    VAR
      line : lengths;
      charsonline : 0 .. maxwidth;

    PROCEDURE NewLine;
    BEGIN
      writeln (outf);    charsonline := 0;
      IF line = bottom THEN
      BEGIN
        page (outf);    line := 1
      END ELSE
        line := line + 1
    END (* New line *);

    PROCEDURE SkipSpaces;
    BEGIN
      WHILE inf^ = ' ' DO
        get (inf)
    END (* Skip spaces *);

    PROCEDURE Space (n : gaps);
    BEGIN
      IF charsonline + n >= margin THEN NewLine ELSE
      BEGIN
        write (outf, ' ' :n);    charsonline := charsonline + n
      END
    END (* Space *);
```

```
PROCEDURE Paragraph;

  PROCEDURE CopyChar;
  BEGIN
    write (outf, inf^);   get (inf);
    charsonline := charsonline + 1
  END (* Copy char *);

  PROCEDURE Sentence;

    PROCEDURE Punctuation;
    BEGIN
      IF inf^ IN [',', ':', ';'] THEN
      BEGIN
        CopyChar;   SkipSpaces
      END
    END (* Punctuation *);

    PROCEDURE Word;
    BEGIN
      REPEAT
        CopyChar
      UNTIL NOT (inf^ IN ['A'..'Z', 'a'..'z', '-', ''''])
    END (* Word *);

  BEGIN (* Sentence *)
    Word;  SkipSpaces;  Punctuation;
    WHILE NOT (inf^ IN ['.', '!', '?']) DO
    BEGIN
      Space (1);   Word;  SkipSpaces;  Punctuation
    END;
    CopyChar
  END (* Sentence *);

  BEGIN (* Paragraph *)
    Sentence;   SkipSpaces;
    WHILE NOT (inf^ IN [parasep, chapterm]) DO
    BEGIN
      Space (2);  Sentence;  SkipSpaces
    END;
    IF inf^ = parasep THEN get (inf)
  END (* Paragraph *);

BEGIN (* Chapter *)
  reset (inf);   rewrite (outf);
  line := 1;   charsonline := 0;   SkipSpaces;
  REPEAT
    Space (5);  Paragraph;  NewLine;  SkipSpaces
  UNTIL inf^ = chapterm;
  get (inf)
END (* Chapter *);

BEGIN (* program body *)
  Chapter (rough, neat, '*', '$', 20, 34)
END.
```

Figure 12.3

The final program is shown in figure 12.3. When this program is run {run number 6}, it transforms the original data file into the following form:

```
          Is this text tidy?
     No, it's a mess!
          Right; what can
     we do about it?  We'll
     write a program to print
     it neatly.
          What a good idea!
```

12.5 Case study 2

We are now going to write a program to output the 'name' of any integer whose absolute magnitude is less than a million. For example, when provided with the value -617489, the program should produce the output

```
     minus six hundred and seventeen thousand
     four hundred and eighty nine
```

Again, you are advised to implement the program yourself as our discussion proceeds. If "maxint" is less than a million on your computer you will have to consider a slightly modified problem: perhaps to output the name of an integer with absolute magnitude less than "maxint".

There are four aspects to this problem. We must produce names corresponding to digits or digit pairs ('six', 'seventeen', 'four', 'eighty', 'nine'), names of powers of ten indicating the weight of each constituent digit group ('hundred', 'thousand'), a possible sign ('minus') and, when appropriate, the word 'and'. We consider each aspect individually and, in accordance with the philosophy outlined earlier, develop our program in stages.

12.5.1 Digit groups

We assume, for the moment, that the number is positive and contains six non-zero digits. We concentrate on the names associated with the digits. To produce these we must determine the appropriate grouping of the digits. In the example above, but ignoring the sign, 617489 splits, first, into two groups: 617 (the number of thousands) and 489 (the number that is left if all the thousands are ignored). So, to name a number less than a million we must be able to name two numbers each less than a thousand. Expressed in programming terms this means that the process

        NameLtMillion (617489)

must be broken down into

        NameLtThousand (617);   NameLtThousand (489)

and so, in general,

        NameLtMillion (n)

becomes

          NameLtThousand (n DIV 1000);   NameLtThousand (n MOD 1000)

To form the appropriate grouping for a three-digit integer we isolate
the first digit (the number of hundreds) and treat the last two as a
pair. The process

          NameLtThousand (617)

must be broken down into

          NameUnit (6);   NameLtHundred (17)

and, in general,

          NameLtThousand (n)

becomes

          NameUnit (n DIV 100);   NameLtHundred (n MOD 100)

     Before we worry about producing names for the digits, let's make
sure that our strategy is correct so far. Figure 12.4 shows a program
which breaks down a six-digit integer into its digit groups. Try it for
yourself {run number 1}. If supplied with the following sequence of
numbers

          617489
          30600
          100001
          203040
          12

the program produces the following output.

          617489 :   6   17   4   89
           30600 :   0   30   6   0
          100001 :   1   0   0   1
          203040 :   2   3   0   40
              12 :   0   0   0   12

Apart from a few superfluous zeros when the number contains zeros or has
fewer than six digits, we see that the grouping is correct. The only
time we use the name 'zero' is when the supplied number is itself 0. We
can treat this as a special case by replacing

          NameLtMillion (n)

in the program body by

          IF n = 0 THEN write ('zero') ELSE
             NameLtMillion (n)

and we can suppress the superfluous zeros by changing the bodies of
"NameUnit" and "NameLtHundred" to

          IF n > 0 THEN write (n :5)

Incorporate these refinements within your program and test them {run
number 2}.

```
PROGRAM NameIntegerRun1 (ints, output);

    (* Breaks a number into its constituent digit groups *)
    CONST
      amillionminus1 = 999999;

    TYPE
      units = 0 .. 9;
      lt100 = 0 .. 99;
      lt1000 = 0 .. 999;
      ltamillion = 0 .. amillionminus1;

    VAR
      ints : text;
      n : ltamillion;

    PROCEDURE NameUnit (n : units);
    BEGIN
      write (n :5)
    END  (* Name Unit *) ;

    PROCEDURE NameLtHundred (n : lt100);
    BEGIN
      write (n :5)
    END  (* Name < 100 *) ;

    PROCEDURE NameLtThousand (n : lt1000);
    BEGIN
      NameUnit (n DIV 100);   NameLtHundred (n MOD 100)
    END  (* Name < 1000 *) ;

    PROCEDURE NameLtMillion (n : ltamillion);
    BEGIN
      NameLtThousand (n DIV 1000);   NameLtThousand (n MOD 1000)
    END  (* Name < 1 000 000 *) ;

BEGIN  (* program body *)
    reset (ints);
    REPEAT
      readln (ints, n);   write (n, ' : ');
      NameLtMillion (n);   writeln
    UNTIL eof (ints)
END.
```

Figure 12.4

As an aside, notice that the identifier "n" has several different
meanings within the program of figure 12.4. At any point, of course,
only one interpretation applies. Within the program body any reference
to "n" implies the variable declared in the outer block but, within a
procedure body, a reference to "n" implies the value that was supplied
as the actual parameter when that particular procedure was called.

12.5.2 Digit group names

If we continue to ignore the weighting of the digit groups we name only
numbers less than 100. We use three sets of names:

```
1 to  9 : the name of the digit
10 to 19 : the name of the digit pair
20 to 99 : the name of the multiple of 10 followed by
           the name of the unit (unless the unit is zero)
```

In programming terms we can define

```
NameLtHundred (n)
```

as

```
IF n < 10 THEN NameUnit (n) ELSE
   IF n < 20 THEN NameTeen (n) ELSE
   BEGIN
      NameTy (n DIV 10);   NameUnit (n MOD 10)
   END
```

The data type

```
teens = 10 .. 19
```

is introduced and the definitions of "NameUnit", "NameTeen" and "NameTy"
are then straightforward. Each uses a case-statement to output the
appropriate name. Try it {run number 3}.

12.5.3 The weights

The points at which a weight must be introduced are apparent from the
initial discussion. For a six-digit number the word 'thousand' must
appear between the two three-digit groups and, for a three-digit number,
the word 'hundred' must appear between the first digit and the remaining
digit pair. This is easily achieved by including appropriate write-
statements within the bodies of "NameLtMillion" and "NameLtThousand".
All is now well provided that the number really does contain six digits
and that the first and fourth are non-zero. In other circumstances we
get inappropriate appearances of the weights. If you don't believe me,
try it! {run number 4}.

     We must modify the program so that the word 'thousand' does not
appear if the number being processed is less than a thousand and the
word 'hundred' does not appear if the number is less than a hundred. We
could modify the body of "NameLtMillion" to

```
IF n >= 1000 THEN
BEGIN
   NameLtThousand (n DIV 1000);   write ('thousand ')
END;
NameLtThousand (n MOD 1000)
```

and make a similar change to "NameLtThousand". This will work but it is
a little illogical. What is the point of evaluating n MOD 1000 when we
have just made a test which can tell us that n is less than 1000? Better
is

```
{1}    IF n < 1000 THEN NameLtThousand (n) ELSE
{2}    BEGIN
{3}       NameLtThousand (n DIV 1000);   write ('thousand ');
{4}       NameLtThousand (n MOD 1000)
{5}    END
```

with a similar approach for "NameLtThousand":

```
IF n < 100 THEN NameLtHundred (n) ELSE
BEGIN
   NameUnit (n DIV 100);   write ('hundred ');
   NameLtHundred (n MOD 100)
END
```

Refine your program accordingly and confirm that no superfluous output appears {run number 5}.

12.5.4 The sign

This is easily accommodated. We process a negative "n" with

```
BEGIN
    write ('minus ');   NameLtMillion (-n)
END
```

and treat non-negative values as previously. Do this {run number 6}.

12.5.5 The word 'and'

This is tricky! Before we can expect our program to print 'and' in the right places we must be clear in our own minds where 'and' should appear. If you try a few examples it should become apparent that 'and' appears only before a number less than 100 and does so if some hundreds or thousands have preceded it. The word 'and' never appears before a unit if the unit is immediately preceded by a non-zero digit or if (in the context of our program) the unit is a number of hundreds.

Right! How do we get this into our program? As usual, we start at the top and work down. The top level of the naming process is the body of "NameLtMillion". When each of the two calls of "NameLtThousand" on lines {1} and {3} produces the name of its parameter we know no 'and' will be needed if the parameter is less than 100. When the call of "NameLtThousand" on line {4} produces the name of its parameter, on the other hand, the word 'and' is needed if its parameter is less than 100. To convey this information to the called procedure we need to supply a second parameter. The body of "NameLtMillion" must take the form

```
IF n < 1000 THEN NameLtThousand (n, no) ELSE
BEGIN
   NameLtThousand (n DIV 1000, no);   write ('thousand ');
   NameLtThousand (n MOD 1000, yes)
END
```

We can write the body of "NameLtMillion" exactly as above if we define

```
        TYPE
          yesorno = (no, yes);
```

and the procedure "NameLtThousand" will take two value parameters:

```
        PROCEDURE NameLtThousand (n : lt1000; andneeded : yesorno);
```

We must modify the body of "NameLtThousand" accordingly. When the value of "andneeded" is "no" its inclusion within the procedure body could be similar to that in "NameLtMillion"

```
        {1}   IF n < 100 THEN NameLtHundred (n, no) ELSE
        {2}   BEGIN
        {3}      NameUnit (n DIV 100, no);   write ('hundred ');
        {4}      NameLtHundred (n MOD 100, yes)
        {5}   END
```

but, if the value of "andneeded" is "yes", we must change the first appearance of "no" to "yes". In other words, the value of the second parameter supplied to "NameLtHundred" on line {1} must be the same as the value of "andneeded". Consequently, we supply "andneeded" as the second parameter in this call.

```
        {1}   IF n < 100 THEN NameLtHundred (n, andneeded) ELSE
        {2}   BEGIN
        {3}      NameUnit (n DIV 100, no);   write ('hundred ');
        {4}      NameLtHundred (n MOD 100, yes)
        {5}   END
```

We now move down one level to "NameLtHundred". We observed earlier that it is only non-zero numbers less than 100 that ever need be preceded by 'and'. Consequently we include, as the first statement of this procedure body,

```
        IF (n <> 0) AND (andneeded = yes) THEN write ('and ')
```

If we were to supply a second parameter to the calls of "NameTy", "NameTeen" and "NameUnit" it would be "no" in each case because none need output the word 'and'. When we considered the body of "NameLtThousand" it was apparent that, if "NameUnit" were to take a second parameter, it would be "no". Since a second parameter supplied to "NameTy", "NameTeen" and "NameUnit" would always be "no", there is no point in having a second parameter. These three procedures need give no consideration to 'and'. The final program has the form shown in Figure 12.5. Test it! {run number 7}.

    As a final observation, notice that our logical approach when avoiding the appearance of superfluous weights paid off. The handling of 'and' would have been less straightforward if we had chosen the approach first suggested when our program would call

```
        NameLtThousand (n MOD 1000)
```

even when n is less than 1000 and

```
        NameLtHundred (n MOD 100)
```

even when n is less than 100.

```
PROGRAM NameIntegerRun7 (input, output);

    (* Prints the name of a supplied integer *)
  CONST
    amillionminus1 = 999999;

  TYPE
    units = 0 ..  9;
    teens = 10 .. 19;

    lt100  = 0 ..  99;
    lt1000 = 0 .. 999;
    ltamillion = 0 .. amillionminus1;
    yesorno = (no, yes);

  VAR
    n : -amillionminus1 .. amillionminus1;

  PROCEDURE NameUnit (n : units);
  BEGIN
    CASE n OF
      0 : ;
      1 : write ('one ');
      2 : write ('two ');
      3 : write ('three ');
      4 : write ('four ');
      5 : write ('five ');
      6 : write ('six ');
      7 : write ('seven ');
      8 : write ('eight ');
      9 : write ('nine ')
    END (* CASE *)
  END (* Name Unit *);

  PROCEDURE NameTeen (n : teens);
  BEGIN
    CASE n OF
      10 : write ('ten ');
      11 : write ('eleven ');
      12 : write ('twelve ');
      13 : write ('thirteen ');
      14 : write ('fourteen ');
      15 : write ('fifteen ');
      16 : write ('sixteen ');
      17 : write ('seventeen ');
      18 : write ('eighteen ');
      19 : write ('nineteen ')
    END (* CASE *)
  END  (* Name Teen *);

  PROCEDURE NameTy (n : units);
  BEGIN
    CASE n OF
      2 : write ('twenty ');
      3 : write ('thirty ');
```

```
          4 : write ('forty ');
          5 : write ('fifty ');
          6 : write ('sixty ');
          7 : write ('seventy ');
          8 : write ('eighty ');
          9 : write ('ninety ')
        END (* CASE *)
      END  (* Name Ty *);

   PROCEDURE NameLtHundred (n : lt100;  andneeded : yesorno);
   BEGIN
     IF (n <> 0) AND (andneeded = yes) THEN
       write ('and ');
     IF n < 10 THEN NameUnit (n) ELSE
       IF n < 20 THEN NameTeen (n) ELSE
       BEGIN
         NameTy (n DIV 10);   NameUnit (n MOD 10)
       END
   END  (* Name < 100 *) ;

   PROCEDURE NameLtThousand (n : lt1000;  andneeded : yesorno);
   BEGIN
     IF n < 100 THEN NameLtHundred (n, andneeded) ELSE
     BEGIN
       NameUnit (n DIV 100);   write ('hundred ');
       NameLtHundred (n MOD 100, yes)
     END
   END  (* Name < 1000 *) ;

   PROCEDURE NameLtMillion (n : ltamillion);
   BEGIN
     IF n < 1000 THEN NameLtThousand (n, no) ELSE
     BEGIN
       NameLtThousand (n DIV 1000, no);   write ('thousand ');
       NameLtThousand (n MOD 1000, yes)
     END
   END  (* Name  < 1 000 000 *) ;

 BEGIN (* program body *)
   write ('Type an integer ');   readln (n);
   IF n > 0 THEN NameLtMillion (n) ELSE
     IF n = 0 THEN write ('zero') ELSE
     BEGIN
       write ('minus ');   NameLtMillion (n)
     END;
   writeln
 END.
```

Figure 12.5

The need for 'and' depends upon whether any previous hundreds or
thousands have been processed. With the illogical constructs this
information is not apparent when these two procedure calls occur. With
our logical approach this information is evident when we need it. The

moral is clear. Always avoid anything illogical. A logical approach makes a program easier to understand, easier to modify later and, as an added bonus, improves overall efficiency.

12.6 Exercises

*1. Implement a simple text editor to edit an external text file. The editor is to copy from one file to another subject to changes specified by commands supplied via "input". Include at least the following commands.

CLn	Copy the next n lines.
CCn	Copy the next n characters (including ends-of-lines).
DLn	Delete the next n lines.
DCn	Delete the next n characters (including ends-of-lines).
Ix...	Insert all text (including ends-of-lines) typed between this occurrence of the character x and the next; x may be any character absent from the text to be inserted.
CE	Copy to the end of the file.
DE	Delete the remainder of the file.
P+	Characters subsequently scanned are to be printed at the terminal.
P-	Characters subsequently scanned are not to be printed at the terminal.
F	Finish.

When your editor is first entered, it should act as though the command P+ has been issued.

2. Write a program to play Blackjack with the program acting as banker and the terminal as a player. Blackjack (pontoon, vingt et un) is played with a standard pack of 52 playing cards and utilises only their denominations. Picture cards are worth 10 points, an ace may be counted as either 1 or 11 points and all other cards are scored at face value.

The banker deals one card to the player and one to himself (face-up). The player places a bet and the banker then deals a second card to the player and a second to himself (face-down). The player's objective is to make the total of points in his hand as close as he can to 21 but without exceeding 21. He does this by 'sticking' (he takes no further cards), 'twisting' (he is dealt one card) or 'buying' (he is dealt one card and he must increase his bet by an amount equal to his original stake). He can twist or buy as many times as he wishes but he cannot buy after twisting; and he may stick whenever he chooses, provided his total does not exceed 21. If his points exceed 21 he is 'bust' and the banker wins the bet.

If the player sticks, the banker must reveal his second card and then must stick if his points total more than 15. If his points do not exceed 15 he must twist until his points exceed 15 or he is bust, whichever is the sooner. If he busts, the player wins the bet; if his point total lies in the range 16 to 21, the hand with the greater number of points wins. In the event of a tie, the banker wins.

   At the end of the round, the cards are retrieved and new hands
dealt. To simplify the computer simulation, assume that the cards
are shuffled prior to each round and ignore the possibility that
more than four cards of the same denomination may be dealt during
one round.

   Your program should keep playing rounds until the player
wishes to stop. The program should impose a maximum stake and must
keep a record of the player's credit. The player can start with a
credit of 0 and, thereafter, a positive credit implies that he is
winning and a negative credit implies that he is losing.

   Initially, value an ace at 11 points and, when the program
performs satisfactorily with this constraint, extend it to accept
the ace's dual role. This can be achieved by counting an ace as 11
points unless the hand busts, whereupon the ace can be devalued to
1 point.

   When your program can play the basic game, extend it to
recognise 'five card tricks' and 'blackjack'. If the player has 21
points with two cards he has 'blackjack' and, unless the banker
also has blackjack, wins the bet. If a hand contains five cards,
this constitutes a 'five card trick'. If the banker has a five card
trick he will stick and this beats anything but blackjack. If the
player has a five card trick then, unless the banker has blackjack
or a five card trick, he wins the bet.

CHAPTER 13
File It

We have written programs to take input from the terminal and to produce output at the terminal; and we have written programs to take input from a previously prepared file and to produce output in a newly created file. These files are text files, containing characters and end of line markers, and are <u>external</u> in that they exist outside the program. In this chapter the notion of files is extended to include files other than text files and <u>internal</u> files which are <u>local</u> to a program. First, we consider local files.

13.1 Local files

At the end of the television series which accompanies this book, a sequence of credits rolls up the screen. If I wanted to produce these credits on paper, I would want each name and title to be in the middle of the page but I would prefer not to have to count all the characters and work out how many spaces to type at the start of each line. I would type everything starting at the left hand margin and write a program to move everything to the right place. Here is a sample data file.

```
        Sound effects
        Honour Matopeer
        Cameraman
        Ivor Lens
        Set construction
        Andy Mann
        Understudy
        Stan Din
        Makeup
        Fay Scream and I Shadow
```

The program must copy each line and centre it within a specified page width. This means that the program will have to read a line and store it somewhere until the number of characters in the line is known. Then the number of spaces needed can be worked out and printed before the line is printed.

The obvious place to keep the line is in a file but the file need not exist outside the program; it is needed only while a line is being copied. We declare the file locally, within the program, and we can process this local file in the same way as an external file; we can rewrite it, reset it, write to it and read from it.

```
    PROGRAM NeatCredits (input, credsource, output, credits);

        (* Centralizes and spaces credits stored
           left-justified as successive lines of a text file *)

        CONST
          maxwidth = 120;    maxgap = 20;
```

```
TYPE
  widths = 1 .. maxwidth;
  gaps = 0 .. maxgap;
VAR
  credsource, credits : text;
  line : 1 .. 2;
  width : widths;
  gap : gaps;

PROCEDURE Centralize (VAR inf, outf : text;  width : widths);
  VAR
    linech : text;
    count : 0 .. maxwidth;
    c : widths;
BEGIN
  rewrite (linech);    count := 0;
  REPEAT
    count := count + 1;
    write (linech, inf^);    get (inf)
  UNTIL eoln (inf);
  readln (inf);    writeln (linech);

  write (outf, ' ' : (width - count) DIV 2);
  reset (linech);
  FOR c := 1 TO count DO
  BEGIN
    write (outf, linech^);    get (linech)
  END;
  writeln (outf)
END (* Centralize *);

PROCEDURE MoveDown (VAR f : text;  n : gaps);
  VAR
    i : gaps;
BEGIN
  FOR i := 1 TO n DO
    writeln (f)
END (* Move down *);

BEGIN (* program body *)
  write (output, 'Pagewidth? ');    readln (input, width);
  write (output, 'Gap size? ');    readln (input, gap);

  reset (credsource);    rewrite (credits);
  REPEAT
    FOR line := 1 TO 2 DO
      Centralize (credsource, credits, width);
    MoveDown (credits, gap)
  UNTIL eof (credsource)
END.
```

Figure 13.1

The   program of figure 13.1 processes a file of credits and, within
the procedure "Centralize", uses a local text file to hold the   incoming
characters   until   the   line length is known. An output file produced by
this program might have the following form.

Costumes
Jim Slip and Leo Tard

Jewellery
T Ara and E R Ring

Vocal harmonies
Su Prano and Barry Tone

Financed by
Robin Banks

As a final note in this section, it must   be   mentioned   that   some
early Pascal compilers do not permit local files.

13.2 General files

There   are two reasons why we often require files other than text files.
One is that there   are   some   things   (values of   symbolic   types,   for
example)   that   cannot   be   stored   directly in a text file; a second is
efficiency. A text file contains characters which we can either   process
one   by   one   or   treat   in groups as numbers. But the computer does not
represent numbers the way we do. In a text file we represent numbers   as
a   sequence   of decimal digits and, perhaps, a decimal point and a minus
sign; but the computer stores numbers in binary. Every   time   a   program
reads   a   number   from   a   text file,   the   computer has to convert the
character form into the internal binary form; and every time   a   program
writes   a   number   to   a   text file, the computer has to convert it back
again. So, if we want to store some values that we don't want to look at
but we want the computer to read again later, we should   store   them   in
the   way the computer wants them – and we can do this with both internal
and external files. We illustrate this with internal files and return to
the examination marks introduced in chapter 6.

        13   A Fool
        97   B A Head
         6   B Hind
        73   I Swotalot
         2   Ivor Thickhead

The first time we met them, we found the mean mark (that is the   average
mark);   this   time   I   want to find the _median_ mark (that is, the middle
mark). For the marks shown above, the median is 13 because two marks are
lower (2 and 6) and two are higher (73 and 97). If there   were   an   even
number   of   marks   we   would   take the median to be the average (perhaps
rounded to an integer) of the middle two marks. If the number   of   marks
(say, n) is odd, the general process for finding the median is

        Remove lowest n DIV 2 marks;
        medmark := smallest left

If the number of marks is even, the general process is

        Remove lowest n DIV 2 marks;
        medmark := average of last removed and smallest left

We can combine these two alternatives conveniently by noting that, in
either case, we remove the lowest (n DIV 2 + 1) marks. If n is odd, the
median is the mark last removed; if n is even, the median is the average
of the last two removed. This algorithm is implemented by the program of
figure 13.2.

```pascal
PROGRAM MedianMark (marksource, output);

    (* Finds the median mark from a file of marks and names *)
    CONST
      maxmark = 100;

    TYPE
      marks = 0 .. maxmark;

    VAR
      marksource : text;
      median : marks;

    PROCEDURE FindMedian
        (VAR marksandnames : text;  VAR medmark : marks);
      CONST
        maxstuds = 250;
      TYPE
        studs = 1 .. maxstuds;
        markfiles = FILE OF marks;
      VAR
        mfile1, mfile2 : markfiles;
        m, n : studs;
        m1, m2 : marks;

      PROCEDURE CountMarks
          (VAR inf : text;
           VAR outf : markfiles;   VAR markcount : studs);
        VAR
          mark : studs;
          count : 0 .. maxstuds;
      BEGIN
        reset (inf);   rewrite (outf);
        count := 0;
        REPEAT
          count := count + 1;
          readln (inf, mark);   write (outf, mark)
        UNTIL eof (inf);
        markcount := count
      END (* Count marks *);

      PROCEDURE RemoveLowest
          (VAR f1, f2 : markfiles;   VAR lowest : marks);
        VAR
          mark, smallest : marks;
      BEGIN
        reset (f1);   rewrite (f2);
        read (f1, smallest);
```

```
          REPEAT
            read (f1, mark);
            IF mark >= smallest THEN write (f2, mark) ELSE
            BEGIN
              write (f2, smallest);    smallest := mark
            END
          UNTIL eof (f1);
          lowest := smallest
        END (* Remove lowest *);

      BEGIN (* Find median *)
        CountMarks (marksandnames, mfile1, n);
        FOR m := 1 TO n DIV 2 + 1 DO
          IF odd (m) THEN
            RemoveLowest (mfile1, mfile2, m1)
          ELSE
            RemoveLowest (mfile2, mfile1, m2);

        IF odd (n) THEN
          CASE odd (n DIV 2 + 1) OF
            true  : medmark := m1;
            false : medmark := m2
          END (* CASE *)
        ELSE
          medmark := (m1 + m2) DIV 2
      END (* Find median *);

    BEGIN (* program body *)
      FindMedian (marksource, median);
      writeln ('Median mark is', median)
    END.
```

Figure 13.2

   To count the marks, the program scans the external text file
containing both marks and names and transfers the marks to an internal
mark file. This is defined to be a file whose <u>component type</u> is "marks"
and so each mark is stored in the file in binary. Once the marks have
been copied to this file, they are repeatedly transferred between this
file and another of the same type and so no binary-decimal conversion
occurs.

   To define a file of component type "t", we use the reserved words
FILE OF. The type declaration

        tfiles = FILE OF t;

defines a type "tfiles" and a variable "tf" of this type would be a file
whose components are of type "t". The file buffer variable "tf^" is a
variable of type "t".

   The procedures "get" and "put", introduced in chapter 5, can be
used with files of any type. The three statements

        f2^ := f1^;   put (f2);   get (f1)

transfer one item from a file "f1" to another file "f2", for any two

files of compatible component type. Some early Pascal compilers forbid
the use of "read" and "write" with anything other than text files and
insist on the use of "get" and "put".

13.3 Merging files

Many applications of computers call for the merging of information from
two files. For example, to add new names to a telephone directory. a
program would take two ordered sequences of names (the existing
directory and the names to be added) and merge them to produce the new
directory. The program of figure 13.3 illustrates the basic process by
applying it to integer files, taking two ascending sequences and merging
them to produce one ascending sequence.

```
PROGRAM Merge (intf1, intf2, intfmerged);

    (* Merges two non-empty integer files *)

  TYPE
    intfiles = FILE OF integer;

  VAR
    intf1, intf2, intfmerged : intfiles;
    state : (merging, atend1, atend2);

  PROCEDURE CopyIntFile (VAR inf, outf : intfiles);
  BEGIN
    WHILE NOT eof(inf) DO
    BEGIN
      write (outf, inf^);   get (inf)
    END
  END (* Copy int file *);

BEGIN (* program body *)
  reset (intf1);   reset (intf2);   rewrite (intfmerged);
  state := merging;
  REPEAT
    IF intf1^ <= intf2^ THEN
    BEGIN
      write (intfmerged, intf1^);   get (intf1);
      IF eof (intf1) THEN state := atend1
    END ELSE
    BEGIN
      write (intfmerged, intf2^);   get (intf2);
      IF eof (intf2) THEN state := atend2
    END
  UNTIL state <> merging;

  CASE state OF
    atend1 : CopyIntFile (intf2, intfmerged);
    atend2 : CopyIntFile (intf1, intfmerged)
  END (* case *)
END.
```

                    Figure 13.3

13.4 Exercises

*1. Write a program to check whether two successive lines of data are identical. The two lines of data are to be typed at the terminal.

*2. Write a program which prints a text file in the form of two columns, the first column containing the first half of the file and the second containing the second half of the file. You may assume that no line in the file is longer than half the width of your output screen.

   Each page of the index to this book was printed by a program which performed this process.

*3. Recast the merging process of figure 13.3 as a procedure and incorporate your procedure in a program to apply a merge sort to four integer files. Each file contains an ascending sequence of integers and the program is to produce a fifth file which combines these four sequences into one ascending sequence.

   You will first have to write a program to construct a binary file of integers, perhaps taking these integers from a text file, and you will also need a program to print a binary file of integers.

4. The procedure "RemoveLowest" of figure 13.2 copies integers from one file to another but for the lowest value present. If this process were repeatedly applied to two files "a" and "b" but in alternate directions (first from a to b, then from b to a, and so on) and the lowest value each time written to a third file "c" then, at the end of the process, the file "c" would contain all the integers in ascending order. Write a program to implement this sorting algorithm.

   Note that the procedure "RemoveLowest" of figure 13.2 assumes that the file it is to read from contains at least two values (because the process is not repeated once half the marks have been removed). This assumption is not valid for the sorting algorithm.

5. Prime numbers in some range 2 to n can be generated by a method known as the 'Sieve of Eratosthenes'. All the integers in the range 2 to n are placed in the sieve and then the primes are listed by repeatedly printing the smallest value in the sieve and removing it and all its multiples from the sieve. The process terminates when the sieve is empty.

   The sieve can be represented as a file of integers and replacement of an integer by 0 can act as 'removal' of the integer.
   a) Write a program which adopts this approach.
   b) Improve your program so that, initially, only odd integers (interspersed with zeros) are placed in the sieve.
   c) Improve your program further so that leading zeros (consecutive zeros at the beginning of the file) are not copied when the file is scanned.

CHAPTER 14
Line Up

An array is effectively a fixed length, random-access local file. In common with a file, an array comprises a linear sequence of components all of the same type. For an array, there are no restrictions upon component type but the length of the sequence is fixed within the type definition. The fundamental difference between arrays and Pascal's sequential files lies in the access mechanisms. The concepts of read-mode and write-mode do not apply to an array and no access order is specified: any element may be accessed (and updated) by reference to its position in the sequence. Positions within the sequence are denoted by a sequence of ordinal values which constitute the index type of the array. One array element corresponds to each value of the index type. At its simplest, an array type definition has the form

```
          ARRAY [ it ] OF ct

where     it is the index type
and       ct is the component type.
```

As already stated, the component type may be any type but the index type must be ordinal. Consider an example:

```
TYPE
    lengths = 28 .. 31;
    months = (jan, feb, mar, apr, may, jun,
              jul, aug, sep, oct, nov, dec);
VAR
    daysin : ARRAY [months] OF lengths;
```

The index type of the array variable "daysin" is "months" and its component type is "lengths". This means that "daysin" comprises twelve variables, each of type "lengths".

The mathematical name for such a construct is vector. Each component variable is identified by indexing (the mathematical term is subscripting) the array: the index (or subscript), enclosed between square brackets, follows the array name. So "daysin [jun]" and "daysin [dec]", for example, are "lengths" variables and can be used just as any other "lengths" variable could be. The two assignments

```
daysin [jun] := 30
```

and

```
daysin [mar] := daysin [jun] + 1
```

are valid.

The power of arrays stems from the fact that a subscript may be any expression whose type is compatible with the declared index type. The assignment

        daysin [succ(nov)] := daysin [pred(pred(may))]

is valid. Naturally, if the index type is a subrange type the value of the subscript must fall within range. For the types

        summermonths = jun .. aug;
        days = 1 .. 31;

and variables

        summerholidaysin : ARRAY [summermonths] OF days

and

        m : months

the expression

        summerholidaysin [m]

is legal. The type of the subscript (m) is "months" and this is compatible with the index type of the array (summermonths) because "summermonths" is a subrange of "months". However, this will be legal at run-time, only if the value of "m" lies in the range jun..aug.

Use of a named type as the index type of an array is not mandatory but is good programming practice. We shall usually adopt this convention.

For our first example, we consider a program to state the number of occurrences of each non-space character in a supplied text file. This entails constructing a table of frequency counts. We must examine each character of the text and, unless it is the space character, increment the appropriate count. The counts must be updated in an unpredictable order and this suggests that they should be stored in an array. The program is in figure 14.1.

Notice how the use of an array governs the choice of the array name. In a context where the entire array is involved (eg the actual parameter "charcounts") choose a name which implies the whole collection of data that the array represents. In a context where reference is made to individual elements (eg the formal parameter "freqof") choose a name which implies a single item of data and invent a suitable name for the subscript (eg "thischar").

As a second example, we shall write a program to print a number in octal. When we write the decimal integer

        74203

this is a shorthand notation for

$$7*10^4 + 4*10^3 + 2*10^2 + 0*10 + 3$$

```
PROGRAM FrequencyCounter (source, counts);

    (* Counts the frequency of occurrence of
       non-space characters in a text file *)
  CONST
    maxcharordnum = 127;

  TYPE
    freqs = 0 .. maxint;
    freqtables = ARRAY [char] OF freqs;

  VAR
    source, counts : text;
    charcounts : freqtables;

  PROCEDURE Construct
      (VAR inf : text;   VAR freqof : freqtables);
      VAR
        thischar : char;
  BEGIN
    FOR thischar := chr(0) TO chr(maxcharordnum) DO
        freqof [thischar] := 0;
    reset (inf);
    WHILE NOT eof (inf) DO
    BEGIN
        read (inf, thischar);
        IF thischar <> ' ' THEN
            freqof [thischar] := freqof [thischar] + 1
    END
  END  (* Construct *) ;

  PROCEDURE Print
      (freqof : freqtables;   VAR outf : text);
      VAR
        thischar : char;
  BEGIN
    rewrite (outf);
    writeln (outf, 'Char   Freq');
    writeln (outf);
    FOR thischar := chr(0) TO chr(maxcharordnum) DO
        IF thischar <> ' ' THEN
            writeln (outf, thischar :3, freqof [thischar] :6)
  END  (* Print *) ;

BEGIN
  Construct (source, charcounts);
  Print (charcounts, outf)
END.
```

Figure 14.1

The decimal system uses base 10 with digits 0, 1, 2, 3, 4, 5, 6, 7, 8
and 9 but numbers can be expressed to any base. In particular, numbers
inside the computer are effectively stored in binary (base 2) with
digits 0 and 1. The octal system uses base 8 and digits 0, 1, 2, 3, 4,
5, 6 and 7. Thus

        74203

in the octal system is equivalent to the decimal value defined by

$$7*8^4 + 4*8^3 + 2*8^2 + 0*8 + 3$$

which is 30851.

        If a positive integer is repeatedly divided by 8, the remainders
are the digits of its octal representation produced in reverse order.
For example

        30851 divided by 8 gives 3856 with remainder 3
         3856 divided by 8 gives 482 with remainder 0
          482 divided by 8 gives   60 with remainder 2
           60 divided by 8 gives   7 with remainder 4
            7 divided by 8 gives   0 with remainder 7

To print a number in octal we can store the remainders as consecutive
elements of an array and then print them in the appropriate order. We
use an array rather than a file because we wish to generate the sequence
in one order and then scan the sequence in the reverse order. The
program is in figure 14.2 and embodies a procedure which has
deliberately been generalized to accept bases other than 8.

14.1 Sorting and searching

Chapter 13 introduced the notion of sorting data using Pascal's
sequential files. The same processes can be applied to arrays but an
array can be sorted in situ (we change the order of entries in the array
without introducing any other arrays) and, because we can access array
elements randomly, we can devise more sophisticated sorting techniques.

14.1.1 Sorting

First we apply the selection sort described in exercise 13.4.4 to an
array. We assume the declarations

        CONST
          tablesize = ... ;
        TYPE
          things = ... ;
          slots = 1 .. tablesize;
          thingtables = ARRAY [slots] OF things;

where "things" is any data type to which the relational operators are
applicable.

```
PROGRAM OctalPrint (input, output);
    (* Converts an integer from decimal to octal *)
TYPE
    bases = 2 .. 10;
    naturals = 0 .. maxint;

VAR
    n : naturals;

PROCEDURE Print (n : naturals;  base : bases);
    CONST
        maxdigitposn = 50;
    VAR
        d : 0 .. maxdigitposn;
        digit : ARRAY [1 .. maxdigitposn] OF 0 .. 9;
    BEGIN
    IF n = 0 THEN write (0 :1) ELSE
    BEGIN
        d := 0;
        REPEAT
            d := d + 1;    digit [d] := n MOD base;
            n := n DIV base
        UNTIL n = 0;

        FOR d := d DOWNTO 1 DO
            write (digit [d] :1)
    END
END  (* Print *) ;

BEGIN  (* program body *)
    writeln ('Give me a non-negative decimal integer ');
    readln (n);
    writeln (n, ' expressed in octal is ');
    Print (n, 8);    writeln
END.
```

Figure 14.2

The overall process, applied to a table "thing" of "n" entries, is

```
FOR i := 1 TO n-1 DO
BEGIN
    { scan elements thing[i], thing[i+1],
            ..., thing[n] and locate the smallest } ;
    { interchange thing[i] with
            the smallest value encountered }
END
```

This expands to give the procedure of figure 14.3.

```
PROCEDURE SelectionSort
     (VAR thing : thingtables;  lastslot : slots);

   VAR
      here, atfront, atminpos : slots;
      atminpos : things;

BEGIN
   FOR atfront := 1 TO lastslot-1 DO
   BEGIN
      min := thing [atfront];   atminpos := atfront;

      FOR here := atfront+1 TO lastslot DO
         IF thing[here] < min THEN
         BEGIN
            min := thing[here];   atminpos := here
         END;

      IF atminpos <> atfront THEN
      BEGIN
         thing[atminpos] := thing[atfront];
         thing[atfront] := min
      END
   END
END  (* Selection Sort *) ;
```

Figure 14.3

One process which, in general, makes fewer scans through the data and fewer entry comparisons is the <u>bubble sort</u>. Scanning the array from left to right, each entry is compared with its neighbour and if two neighbouring entries are 'the wrong way round' they are interchanged. This has the effect of moving the largest value to the right hand end (it 'bubbles' to the top) and improving the relative ordering of the smaller values. For example, if we wish to sort the sequence

47 26 58 41 17 94 52

into ascending order,

47 swaps with 26
58 swaps with 41
58 swaps with 17
94 swaps with 52

giving the sequence

26 47 41 17 58 52 94

We repeat this process, but scanning one entry fewer each time, until a scan produces no interchanges. The sequence is then in order. For the present example the sequences produced by successive scans are as follows.

```
47 26 58 41 17 94 52
26 47 41 17 58 52    94
26 41 17 47 52    58 94
26 17 41 47    52 58 94
17 26 41    47 52 58 94
   17 26 41 47 52 58 94
```

Each enlarged gap indicates the point at which a scan terminated.

The process is applied to a table of "things" by the procedure of figure 14.4. This procedure can be made more efficient and an exercise at the end of this chapter encourages this.

```
PROCEDURE BubbleSort
    (VAR thing : thingtables;  lastslot : slots);
  VAR
    changed : boolean;
    here, endofscan : slots;
    this : things;
BEGIN
  endofscan := lastslot;
  REPEAT
    endofscan := endofscan - 1;   changed := false;
    FOR here := 1 TO endofscan DO
      IF thing [here] > thing [here+1] THEN
      BEGIN
        this := thing [here];   thing [here] := thing [here+1];
        thing [here+1] := this;   changed := true
      END
  UNTIL NOT changed OR (endofscan=1)
END   (* Bubble Sort *) ;
```

Figure 14.4

14.1.2 Searching

When searching an unordered array, a simple linear search can be applied. The procedure of figure 14.5 does this. If the desired entry is located, "found" is given the value "true" and "posn" indicates its position within the array.

If we wish to search a table whose entries are ordered we can devise more sophisticated techniques. One is called binary chopping because we repeatedly 'chop the table in half'. We first examine the middle entry (or, if the table contains an even number of entries, one of the middle two entries). If this is the value we seek we terminate the search; if not, we compare it with the value we seek. Because the elements of the array are ordered, the comparison tells us which half of the sequence will contain the desired value, if it is present. If the

---

```
PROCEDURE FindByLinearSearch
    (thingwanted : things;  thing : thingtables;  lastslot : slots;
     VAR posn : slots;  VAR found : boolean);

  VAR
    here : slots;
    state : (seeking, gotit, givenup);

BEGIN
  here := 1;   state := seeking;
  REPEAT
    IF thing [here] = thingwanted THEN state := gotit ELSE
      IF here = lastslot THEN state := givenup ELSE
        here := here + 1
  UNTIL state <> seeking;

  IF state = gotit THEN
  BEGIN
    found := true;   posn := here
  END ELSE
    found := false
END  (* Find by Linear Search *) ;
```

Figure 14.5

---

desired value is less than the value currently examined it must lie in
the first half; if not, it must lie in the second. We apply the same
approach to the appropriate half of the table and repeat this process,
considering a smaller section of the table each time until either we
locate the desired entry or _exhaust_ the search (we have chopped the
table so much that there is nothing left!)

The procedure of figure 14.6 applies the binary chopping process to
search an ordered table of "things".

The expected number of accesses needed to locate an arbitrary entry
within a sequence of length n is of the order of n/2 for linear search
and of the order of $\log_2 n$ for binary chopping. As n gets larger, so does
the difference between n/2 and $\log_2 n$. The saving achieved by binary
chopping is highlighted by considering a few sample values.

n	n/2	$\log_2 n$
2	1	1
8	4	3
32	16	5
128	64	7
1024	512	10
32768	16384	15

```
PROCEDURE FindByBinaryChopping
   (thingwanted : things;  thingat : thingtables;  lastslot : slots;
   VAR posn : slots;    VAR found : boolean);

  VAR
    bottom, middle, top : slots;
    state : (stillchopping, gotit, givenup);

BEGIN
  IF (thingwanted < thingat[1]) OR
     (thingwanted > thingat[lastslot]) THEN found := false ELSE
  BEGIN
    bottom := 1;   top := lastslot;   state := stillchopping;

    REPEAT
      middle := (top + bottom) DIV 2;
      IF thingat[middle] = thingwanted THEN state := gotit ELSE
        IF top <= bottom THEN state := givenup ELSE
          IF thingwanted < thingat[middle] THEN
            top := middle - 1
          ELSE
            bottom := middle + 1
    UNTIL state <> stillchopping;

    found := state = gotit;
    IF found THEN posn := middle
  END
END  (* Find by Binary Chopping *) ;
```

Figure 14.6

14.2 Packed arrays and strings

Consider the following data types.

```
months = (jan, feb, mar, apr, may, jun,
          jul, aug, sep, oct, nov, dec);
days = 1 .. 31;
dates = ARRAY [months] OF days;
```

Within the computer, an object of type "dates" will occupy 12 locations, one for each month. Most of the space inside these locations will be unused so storage would be saved if more than one value were packed into each location. Typically, each location (called a word) in a small computer holds sixteen binary digits (abbreviated to "bits") and, in a large computer, possibly as many as sixty. The binary equivalent of 31 is 11111 so only five bits are needed to represent a value in the range 1 to 31. This means that, for a 16-bit machine, we could store three "days" per word and, for a 60-bit machine, twelve "days" per word. The storage required for a "dates" object would then be reduced from twelve words to four words in a 16-bit machine and to only one word in a 60-bit machine.

14.2.1 Packed arrays

We achieve this economisation of space by preceding the word ARRAY by the word PACKED in the array definition.

        dates = PACKED ARRAY [months] OF days;

Of course, we must pay some price for the increased storage efficiency! We do so by way of a time penalty every time we access an element of a packed array because each element we require must be unpacked. Use of a packed array is advisable when the array is referred to bodily (passed as a value parameter or assigned bodily) with perhaps occasional references to individual elements, but not if repeated reference is being made to elements.

    Pascal provides two procedures to convert between packed and unpacked forms. For two arrays

        a : ARRAY [b1 .. b2] OF t;
        pa : PACKED ARRAY [pb1 .. pb2] OF t;

with identical component type "t", the statement

        pack (a, i, pa)

packs successive elements a[i], a[succ(i)], ... into "pa" until "pa" is full, and the statement

        unpack (pa, a, i)

unpacks the whole of "pa" into successive elements a[i], a[succ(i)], ... Consequent constraints are that the array "a" must not be declared to have fewer elements than "pa" and "i" must be in the range "b1" to "b2" and such that processing does not 'fall off the end of' "a". Expressed mathematically, the constraint on "a" is

        ord (b1) <= ord (i) <= ord (b2) − ord (pb2) + ord (pb1)

14.2.2 Strings

One particular application of packed arrays is to represent strings. A packed array whose component type is "char" and index type is an integer subrange with lower bound 1 is said to be a string. A string of the form we met in chapter 1 and containing n characters is a constant of the type

        PACKED ARRAY [1 .. n] OF char

and so could be assigned to a variable of identical type. In the scope of the variable declaration

        message : PACKED ARRAY [1 .. 7] OF char;

the assignment

        message := 'Goodbye'

is legal. A string variable may be supplied as a parameter to "write" or "writeln" and so, after the above assignment, the statement

        writeln (message, ' Fred')

would produce the output

Goodbye Fred

To assign a string of fewer than seven characters, we would include spaces to make the number up to seven:

message := 'Hello '

All the relational operators can be applied to two strings of identical type. A test such as

IF message > 'Bye   ' THEN ...

is legal and compares the lexicographic ordering of the two strings. This extends the concept of alphabetic ordering to include all the members of the available character set.

For an example involving strings, we return to our file of examination marks and names. Given a student's name, the program of figure 14.7 finds that student's mark. It assumes that no name will contain more than twenty characters.

14.3 Array parameters

A scalar parameter of a routine (a parameter of type boolean, char, integer, symbolic, subrange or real) should be passed as a value parameter if the routine is interested only in its value (ie it is an input parameter) and as a variable parameter if the routine requires the ability to change its current value (ie it is an output parameter). Unless your compiler provides very generous sets this will also apply to set parameters. Ideally, the same logic should apply to arrays. Unfortunately, there is a drawback. Transfer of a value parameter involves the construction of a local copy each time the routine is called. If the parameter is a large array, this can be a costly process in terms of both time and space. Transfer of a variable parameter, however, entails only the setting up of a pointer to the actual parameter. Consequently, for reasons of efficiency, an array is usually transferred as a variable parameter unless we know that the array will be very small or we really do want a local copy constructing when the routine is called (see figure 15.10 for an example of this).

```
PROGRAM GetMark (input, marksource, output);

     (* Retrieves a student's examination mark *)

   CONST
     maxnamelength = 20;    maxmark = 100;

   TYPE
     marks = 0 .. maxmark;
     names = PACKED ARRAY [1..maxnamelength] OF char;

   VAR
     marksource : text;
     name : names;
     mark : marks;
     gotit : boolean;
```

```
      PROCEDURE ReadName (VAR f : text;    VAR namech : names);
         CONST
            spaces20 = '                         ';
         VAR
            c : 0 .. maxnamelength;
      BEGIN
         WHILE f^ = ' ' DO
            get (f);
         namech := spaces20;    c := 0;
         REPEAT
            c := c + 1;    read (f, namech [c])
         UNTIL eoln (f);
         readln (f)
      END (* Read name *);

      PROCEDURE FindMark
            (VAR inf : text;    namewanted : names;
             VAR markwanted : marks;    VAR success : boolean);
         VAR
            thismark : marks;
            thisname : names;
            state : (looking, found, atendoffile);
      BEGIN
         reset (inf);    state := looking;
         REPEAT
            read (inf, thismark);    ReadName (inf, thisname);
            IF thisname = namewanted THEN state := found ELSE
               IF eof (inf) THEN state := atendoffile
         UNTIL state <> looking;
         success := state = found;
         IF success THEN markwanted := thismark
      END (* Find mark *);

   BEGIN (* program body *)
      writeln (output, 'Name? ');    ReadName (input, name);
      FindMark (marksource, name, mark, gotit);
      IF gotit THEN
         writeln ('Mark is', mark)
      ELSE
         writeln ('Name (', name, ') not found')
   END.
```

                         Figure 14.7

14.4 Exercises

1. (i) Write a procedure to read a word and print it backwards.
         Assume that the word will contain only letters.
    (ii) Incorporate this procedure within a program to reverse every
         word in a sentence. Assume the sentence contains no
         punctuation other than a full stop immediately following the
         last word.

*2. A palindrome is a word or phrase which reads the same backwards as forwards if spaces and punctuation are ignored. "Madam, I'm Adam" is a well-known example. Write a program which reads a phrase, typed on one line, and determines whether it is palindromic.

3. Write a program to determine if one word is an anagram of another. {Hint: compare the frequency count of each letter of each word.}

*4. Exercise 13.4.5 described the use of the 'Sieve of Eratosthenes' to produce prime numbers up to some bound, n. Supply n as a user-defined constant and, representing the sieve by a boolean array, write a program to produce all the prime numbers in the range 1 to n.

*5. Write a program to produce Pascal's triangle of binomial coefficients as far as those for some power, specified as a user-defined constant. Each number, other than 1, is the sum of the two numbers immediately above it. The triangle below gives coefficients up to the power of six.

```
            1
          1   1
        1   2   1
      1   3   3   1
    1   4   6   4   1
  1   5  10  10   5   1
1   6  15  20  15   6   1
```

6. An integer outside the range [-maxint, maxint] can be represented by recording its sign and storing its digits in successive elements of an array. Adopting such a scheme and imposing some limit upon the length of an integer, write one procedure to read a long integer, one to write a long integer and three to process a pair of long integers:
   one to form their sum,
   one to form their difference, and
   one to form their product.
Incorporate these within a program to read four long integers a, b, c, d and print the values ab+cd and ab-cd.

7. Assuming n is a power of 2, the following algorithm sorts n items into order. First, consider successive pairs and interchange values if necessary so that values in each pair are in order. Then consider successive groups of four and rearrange values if necessary so that values in each group of four are in order. Continue this process, doubling the size of the group each time, until the full set is ordered.

   This is effectively a merge sort (see section 13.3) applied to elements of an array. If the process is applied to the eight integers

   37   17   94   32   12   97   82   31

and ascending order is desired, the ordering at the end of successive scans is as follows.

```
Scan 1:  17  37  32  94  12  97  31  82   (group size 2)
Scan 2:  17  32  37  94  12  31  82  97   (group size 4)
Scan 3:  12  17  31  32  37  82  94  97   (group size 8)
```

a) Write a program implementing this algorithm to sort a set of integers into ascending order. The simplest approach is to use two arrays and copy from one to the other during each scan, but the sort can be implemented in situ in one array.

b) Modify your program so that it caters for any positive value of n (and is not restricted to powers of 2).

8. Improve the efficiency of the bubble sort procedure of figure 14.4. A complete scan of the sequence
    15 20 25 30 35 10 40 60 45 55 50 65 70 75
produces the sequence
    15 20 25 30 10 35 40 45 55 50 60 65 70 75
This indicates three areas of possible improvement.

(i) Because the largest value always 'bubbles to the top' there is no need to scan beyond the last value brought down (moved left) during the previous scan. In the example, the last value brought down is 50 and there is no need for any subsequent scan to extend beyond this 50.

(ii) Because a value cannot move down more than one place during a scan there is no need to start a scan any lower than one below the first value moved down during the previous scan. In the example, the first value moved down is 10 and there is no need to start the next scan before 30, the value currently immediately below 10.

(iii) A value often moves up more than one place during a scan. In the example above, 60 moves up three places. The procedure of figure 14.4 will
      swap 60 and 45
      then 60 and 55
    and then 60 and 50.
This process would be faster if 45, 55 and 50 were moved down and 60 then inserted where 50 had been. The overall process would be speeded up even more if the 45, 55 and 50 were partially ordered while they were being moved.

*9. Write a program which checks whether the first n characters on one line of data are the same as the first n on the next; n is a user-defined constant. Store the first n characters on each line as a string.

*10. Write a program to count the number of occurrences of a given word in a piece of text. The text is stored in a file and the sought word is supplied from the keyboard.

CHAPTER 15
New Dimensions

It has already been mentioned that the element type of an array can, itself, be an array type. This gives what is called a <u>multi-dimensional</u> structure. Assuming the existence of two constants

```
firstyear = 1976;
lastyear  = 1980;
```

consider the following types.

```
months = (jan, feb, mar, apr, may, jun,
          jul, aug, sep, oct, nov, dec);
years = firstyear .. lastyear;
yearlyrains = ARRAY [months] OF real;
raintables = ARRAY [years] OF yearlyrains;
```

The data type "raintables" represents a two-dimensional table with five rows (labelled 1976, 1977, ..., 1980) and twelve columns (labelled jan, feb, ..., dec). You can, if you prefer, regard this table as having five columns and twelve rows but the interpretation suggested is customary.

In the scope of the following variables

```
rain : raintables;
   m : months;
   y : years;
```

we could have the following subscripted expressions.

```
rain [y]      of type yearlyrains
rain [y][m]   of type real
```

Because a multi-dimensional array is often supplied with more than one subscript, Pascal provides a shorthand notation: the reversed bracket pair "][" may be replaced by a comma.

```
rain [y, m]   is equivalent to   rain [y][m]
```

If no intermediate named types are required, a similar shorthand notation may be used for array declarations. The variable "rain" represents the same two-dimensional structure if "raintables" is the type

```
ARRAY [years, months] OF real
```

but now the expression

```
rain [y]
```

is of limited use because it has no explicit type.

A common example of two-dimensional arrays is a table of strings, perhaps people's names. This would be the case in section 14.1 if the data type "things", introduced in section 14.1.1, were a string type. Notice that, because relational operators are applicable to strings, the sort and search procedures of section 14.1 can be applied to a table of strings. To illustrate general processing of two-dimensional arrays we consider three routines concerned with "raintables" as defined above.

1. A procedure to determine the wettest month of the recorded period.

We must scan the entire table to locate the maximum value it contains and note the corresponding year and month. We can scan the entire table with a loop of the form

```
FOR y := firstyear TO lastyear DO
   { examine each rainfall figure for year y }
```

or a loop of the form

```
FOR m := jan TO dec DO
  ·{ examine each rainfall figure for month m }
```

The first gives <u>row-wise</u> scanning (all the months of the first year are examined before any subsequent year is considered) and the second gives <u>column-wise</u> scanning (the same month is examined for every year before the next month is considered). Each can be expanded by including a second loop. For row-wise scanning we get

```
FOR y := firstyear TO lastyear DO
   FOR m := jan TO dec DO
      { examine rain[y,m] }
```

and, for column-wise scanning,

```
FOR m := jan TO dec DO
   FOR y := firstyear TO lastyear DO
      { examine rain[y,m] }
```

Row-wise scanning is usually more natural, and is so in this case, so we shall adopt it.

As we scan the table we must keep a record of the maximum value so far encountered and note its location. When we examine each particular value rain[y,m] we must compare it with the maximum so far and, if necessary, update our record of the maximum.

```
IF rain [y, m] > maxsofar THEN
BEGIN
   maxsofar := rain [y, m];
   wety := y;   wetm := m
END
```

We must ensure that, before entry to the nested loops, the variables "wety", "wetm" and "maxsofar" are suitably initialized. We could initialize them to record the first value in the table (the entry in the first column of the first row)

```
wety := firstyear;   wetm := jan;
maxsofar := rain [firstyear, jan]
```

but, more simply, we need only give "maxsofar" a value less than any that can be encountered in the table (say, -1). This ensures that the first application of the test

        rain [y, m] > maxsofar

(when y = firstyear and m = jan) will produce the value "true" and then the desired initialization of "wety", "wetm" and "maxsofar" will be achieved. The complete procedure is in figure 15.1.

```
        PROCEDURE FindWettestMonth
                (rain : raintables;
                 VAR month : months;    VAR year : years);

            VAR
                maxsofar : real;
                m, wetm : months;
                y, wety : years;
        BEGIN
            maxsofar := -1;
            FOR y := firstyear TO lastyear DO
                FOR m := jan TO dec DO
                    IF rain [y, m] > maxsofar THEN
                    BEGIN
                        maxsofar := rain [y, m];    wety := y;    wetm := m
                    END;
            year := wety;    month := wetm
        END (* Find wettest month *) ;
```

                            Figure 15.1

        If we adopt row-wise scanning we can perform a process known as slicing. The action

        { examine each rainfall figure for year y }

can be performed by a routine which takes rain[y] as a parameter (of type "yearlyrains"); a row is sliced from the table and passed to a routine. The procedure of figure 15.2 does this. The advantage of this approach is that no doubly subscripted expressions occur and access to an array element is faster the fewer subscripts are needed to identify it. Also transparency may be improved. A disadvantage is that this involves the overhead of a routine call and the transfer of its parameters. In practice, the contribution of slicing to efficiency will depend upon the run-time subscripting saved. In the present case it probably makes little difference but where elements of a row are accessed many times the saving can be considerable.

        As mentioned in section 14.3, time can often be saved by transferring array parameters as variables rather than as values and this is particularly so with two-dimensional arrays, which tend to be larger than one-dimensional arrays. However, promoting efficiency at the expense of security, transparency and aesthetic programming style is not the aim of this book so we shall ignore this consideration and use variable parameters only where necessary.

```
PROCEDURE FindWettestMonth
        (rain : raintables;
         VAR month : months;  VAR year : years);

    VAR
        fall, maxsofar : real;
        wetm, wetmonth : months;
        thisyear, wetyear : years;

    PROCEDURE GetWettestMonthThisYear
            (raininmonth : yearlyrains;
             VAR month : months;  VAR fallinthismonth : real);
        VAR
            maxyet : real;
            m, wetm : months;
    BEGIN
        maxyet := -1;
        FOR m := jan TO dec DO
            IF raininmonth [m] > maxyet THEN
            BEGIN
                wetm := m;   maxyet := raininmonth [m]
            END;
        month := wetm;   fallinthismonth := maxyet
    END (* Get wettest month this year *) ;

  BEGIN  (* Find wettest month *)
    maxsofar := -1;
    FOR thisyear := firstyear TO lastyear DO
    BEGIN
        GetWettestMonthThisYear (rain [thisyear], wetm, fall);
        IF fall > maxsofar THEN
        BEGIN
            wetmonth := wetm;   wetyear := thisyear;   maxsofar := fall
        END
    END;
    year := wetyear;   month := wetmonth
  END  (* Find wettest month *) ;
```

Figure 15.2

---

2. A function to determine which month of the year was the wettest on
average.

The month which is the wettest on average will be that month with the
highest accumulated rainfall for the whole period. We need to scan the
columns of our table. The function is in figure 15.3.

3. A function to deliver the wettest year.

We need to scan the rows of our table. Figure 15.4 shows a function
which achieves this with slicing.

```
FUNCTION monthwithmaxtotal (rain : raintables) : months;
   VAR
      month, wettestmonth : months;
      monthsrain, mostrainsofar : real;

   FUNCTION totalin (m : months) : real;
      VAR
         y : years;
         total : real;
   BEGIN
      total := 0;
      FOR y := firstyear TO lastyear DO
         total := total + rain [y, m];
      totalin := total
   END  (* total in *) ;

BEGIN  (* month with max total *)
   mostrainsofar := -1;
   FOR month := jan TO dec DO
   BEGIN
      monthsrain := totalin (month);
      IF monthsrain > mostrainsofar THEN
      BEGIN
         mostrainsofar := monthsrain;
         wettestmonth := month
      END
   END;
   monthwithmaxtotal := wettestmonth
END  (* month with max total *) ;
```

                    Figure 15.3

15.1 Vectors and matrices

Arrays provide a natural representation of the mathematician's vectors
and matrices.

```
CONST
   n = ... ;   m = ... ;

TYPE
   oneton = 1 .. n;   onetom = 1 .. m;

   nvectors = ARRAY [oneton] OF real;
   mvectors = ARRAY [onetom] OF real;

   nbym = ARRAY [oneton] OF mvectors;
   mbyn = ARRAY [onetom] OF nvectors;
   nbyn = ARRAY [oneton] OF nvectors;
```

```
FUNCTION yearwithmaxtotal (rain : raintables) : years;

    VAR
        y, wetyear : years;
        yearsrain, maxyet : real;

    FUNCTION totalinyear (raininmonth : yearlyrains) : real;
    VAR
        m : months;
        total : real;
    BEGIN
        total := 0;
        FOR m := jan TO dec DO
            total := total + raininmonth [m];
        totalinyear := total
    END  (* total in year *) ;

BEGIN  (* year with max total *)
    maxyet := -1;
    FOR y := firstyear TO lastyear DO
    BEGIN
        yearsrain := totalinyear (rain [y]);
        IF yearsrain > maxyet THEN
        BEGIN
            maxyet := yearsrain;   wetyear := y
        END
    END;
    yearwithmaxtotal := wetyear
END  (* year with max total *) ;
```

Figure 15.4

We consider the computation of
    1. the dot product of two vectors,
    2. the cross product of two vectors,
    3. the transpose of a matrix and
    4. the product of two matrices.

1. In the usual mathematical notation, the dot (or scalar) product of two n-vectors **u** and **v** is

$$\mathbf{u}.\mathbf{v} = \sum_{i=1}^{n} u_i v_i$$

The function of figure 15.5 computes the dot product.

2. The cross (or vector) product of an n-vector **u** and an m-vector **v** is the n by m matrix **A** defined such that $A_{ij} = u_i v_j$. The procedure of figure 15.6 forms a cross product.

```
FUNCTION dotproduct (u, v : nvectors) : real;
   VAR
      i : oneton;
      sum : real;
BEGIN
   sum := 0;
   FOR i := 1 TO n DO
      sum := sum + u[i] * v[i];
   dotproduct := sum
END  (* dot product *) ;
```

Figure 15.5

```
PROCEDURE FormCrossProduct
      (u : nvectors;  v : mvectors;  VAR a : nbym);
   VAR
      i : oneton;    j : onetom;
BEGIN
   FOR i := 1 TO n DO
      FOR j := 1 TO m DO
         a[i,j] := u[i] * v[j]
END  (* Form cross product *) ;
```

Figure 15.6

---

3. The transpose of a matrix **A** is a matrix **B** such that $B_{ij} = A_{ji}$. If we wish to retain the original matrix we must have a second array available in which to produce the transpose. The procedure of figure 15.7 produces, in one array, the transpose of another.

```
PROCEDURE FormTranspose (a : nbym;  VAR atran : mbyn);
   VAR
      i : oneton;    j : onetom;
BEGIN
   FOR i := 1 TO n DO
      FOR j := 1 TO m DO
         atran [i,j] := a [j,i]
END  (* Form transpose *) ;
```

Figure 15.7

If the original matrix is square and is to be replaced by its transpose we can perform the transposition in situ. Figure 15.8 illustrates this.

```
PROCEDURE Transpose (VAR a : nbyn);
   VAR
      i, j : oneton;
      aij : real;
BEGIN
   FOR i := 1 TO n-1 DO
      FOR j := i+1 TO n DO
      BEGIN  (* swap a[i,j] and a[j,i] *)
         aij := a[i,j];   a[i,j] := a[j,i];   a[j,i] := aij
      END
END  (* Transpose *) ;
```

Figure 15.8

---

4. The product of two matrices **A** (n by m) and **B** (m by n) is a matrix
C (n by n) defined such that the element C_{ij} is the dot product of the
i^{th} row-vector of **A** with the jth column-vector of **B**.

$$C_{ij} = \sum_{k=1}^{m} A_{ik}B_{kj}$$

Ignoring the possibility of slicing, the procedure of figure 15.9 models
a solution directly on this formula.

```
PROCEDURE FormProduct
      (a : nbym;   b : mbyn;   VAR c : nbyn);
   VAR
      i, j : oneton;
      k : onetom;
      sum : real;
BEGIN
   FOR i := 1 TO n DO
      FOR j := 1 TO n DO
      BEGIN
         sum := 0;
         FOR k := 1 TO m DO
            sum := sum + a[i,k] * b[k,j];
         c[i,j] := sum
      END
END  (* Form product *) ;
```

Figure 15.9

We can slice "a" to produce its ith row "a[i]", but we cannot
directly extract the jth column of "b". The neatest solution arises if
the transpose **B'** of **B** is available. The value C_{ij} is then the dot

product of the ith row-vector of **A** with the jth row-vector of **B'** and so
we can use our earlier function to evaluate a dot product. We could of
course transpose **B** inside the product procedure but this extra
computation would produce an inefficient solution. Nevertheless, to
illustrate the technique, the procedure of figure 15.10 does this for
square matrices and performs the transformation in situ.

```
    PROCEDURE FormSquareProduct (a, b : nbyn;  VAR c : nbyn);
      VAR
          i, j : oneton;
    BEGIN
      Transpose (b);
      FOR i := 1 TO n DO
        FOR j := 1 TO n DO
            c[i,j] := dotproduct (a[i], b[j])
      END  (* Form square product *) ;
```

                        Figure 15.10

Notice that "b" is transferred as a value parameter. This is so that a
local copy will be constructed and it is this local copy which is
transposed; the actual parameter remains uncorrupted.

15.2 Drawing pictures

If your implementation permits a Pascal program to control cursor
movement you can use this facility to draw a picture on the terminal
screen. But what if we want to produce the picture on some other device
which does not have a screen, or perhaps store the picture in a file for
subsequent printing? Then we have to produce the picture as lines of
characters stored in a text file.

        It is possible to write a program which draws a picture simply by
using lots of writeln-statements. The trouble with this approach is that
you have to draw your picture from the top down to the bottom and, if
you want to change your picture a little, you may have to change your
program a lot.

        An alternative approach is to use an array to represent the screen.
We can build a picture up inside the array in any order we like and then
print the array from the top to the bottom when the picture is finished.
To refer to points on the screen, we can use a two-dimensional
coordinate system with an x-axis running horizontally across the screen
from left to right and a y-axis running vertically up the screen.
Typically, a terminal can display 79 characters on a line before the
cursor moves to the next line (which happens when the 80th character is
printed) and can display 23 lines on the screen before the top line is
pushed off. So, to represent the coordinate system in a Pascal program,
we might use a two-dimensional array type with index types 0..78 and
0..22.

```
CONST
  maxx = 78;    maxy = 22;
TYPE
  xcoords = 0 .. maxx;
  ycoords = 0 .. maxy;
  screens = ARRAY [xcoords, ycoords] OF char;
```

In the previous examples we used the first dimension to identify a row and the second to identify a column; but now we are doing things the other way round. This time we think of the first dimension as identifying a column and the second dimension as identifying a row. It does not matter which way we choose to interpret the two dimensions so long as we are consistent; if we start off thinking the first dimension represents a column, then we must stick to that interpretation.

To illustrate the process of constructing a picture we shall take something very simple: a van.

```
            ************************
            *                      *
            *                      *
            *                      *
       ******                      *
       *    *                      *
       *    *                      *
       ****************************
         **                  **
```

The basic process comprises three steps. First we clear the array that we are using to represent the screen, then build up the picture inside the array and, finally, display the picture by printing the array at the terminal. The program of figure 15.11 will produce the van shown above. The program draws two rectangles (the van body and the engine compartment) and two squares (the wheels). The engine compartment length ("ecl") is taken to be approximately one fifth of the overall length and its height is taken to be half the height of the van body. The wheel size is taken to be approximately a third of the length of the engine compartment.

To draw the four sides of a rectangle, the program obeys four calls of a procedure to draw a line. This procedure takes as parameters the x and y coordinates of one end of the line, the length of the line and the direction one must travel to reach the other end of the line. For a rectangle or square, four directions suffice (in fact, two would suffice) but this technique can be extended for more complicated shapes.

```
PROGRAM Vans (input, output);

    (* Draws a picture of a van *)

CONST
  maxx = 78;    maxy = 22;
```

```
TYPE
  xcoords = 0 .. maxx;
  ycoords = 0 .. maxy;
  dists = xcoords;   (* larger of xcoords and ycoords *)
  screens = ARRAY [xcoords, ycoords] OF char;

VAR
  screen : screens;

PROCEDURE Clear (VAR charat : screens);
  VAR
    x : xcoords;   y : ycoords;
BEGIN
  FOR x := 0 TO maxx DO
    FOR y := 0 TO maxy DO
      charat [x, y] := ' '
END (* Clear *);

PROCEDURE Display (charat : screens);
  VAR
    x : xcoords;   y : ycoords;
BEGIN
  FOR y := maxy DOWNTO 0 DO
  BEGIN
    FOR x := 0 TO maxx DO
      write (charat [x, y]);
    writeln
  END
END (* Display *);

PROCEDURE DrawVan
    (VAR spot : screens;   bfx : xcoords;   bfy : ycoords;
     length : xcoords;   height : ycoords);
  VAR
    bodylength, ecl, wheel : xcoords;

  PROCEDURE DrawRectangle
      (x : xcoords;   y : ycoords;
       w : xcoords;   h : ycoords);
    (* x, y are the coordinates of
       the bottom left hand corner *)
    TYPE
      dirns = (right, left, up, down);

    PROCEDURE DrawLine
        (x : xcoords;   y : ycoords;
         dirn : dirns;   dist : dists);
      CONST
        bright = '*';
      VAR
        d : dists;
        xinc, yinc : -1 .. 1;
    BEGIN (* Draw Line *)
      CASE dirn OF
        right : BEGIN
                  xinc := 1;   yinc := 0
                END;
```

```
            left : BEGIN
                       xinc := -1;    yinc := 0
                   END;
              up : BEGIN
                       xinc := 0;    yinc := 1
                   END;
            down : BEGIN
                       xinc := 0;    yinc := -1
                   END
        END (* CASE *);
        spot [x, y] := bright;
        FOR d := 2 TO dist DO
        BEGIN
          x := x + xinc;    y := y + yinc;
          spot [x, y] := bright
        END
      END (* Draw line *);

   BEGIN (* Draw rectangle *)
     DrawLine (x, y, right, w);
     DrawLine (x+w-1, y, up, h);
     DrawLine (x+w-1, y+h-1, left, w);
     DrawLine (x, y+h-1, down, h)
   END (* Draw rectangle *);

  BEGIN (* Draw van *)
    ecl := round (length / 5);
    bodylength := length - ecl + 1;
    wheel := round (ecl/3);
    (* Draw engine compartment *)
    DrawRectangle (bfx, bfy, ecl, height DIV 2);
    (* Draw van body *)
    DrawRectangle (bfx+ecl-1, bfy, bodylength, height);
    (* Draw wheels *)
    DrawRectangle (bfx+wheel, bfy-wheel+1, wheel, wheel);
    DrawRectangle (bfx+bodylength, bfy-wheel+1, wheel, wheel)
  END (* Draw van *);

BEGIN (* program body *)
  Clear (screen);
  DrawVan (screen, 10, 3, 28, 8);
  Display (screen)
END.
```

Figure 15.11

15.3 Exercises

*1. A text file contains, at most, a hundred names, each containing no more than thirty characters and each preceded by a different reference number, an integer in the range 0 to 99. Write a program to produce a file containing the supplied names and numbers but in descending order of reference number. By using a suitable array of names, your program should achieve this without the need for a sorting process such as those described in section 14.1.

*2. Write procedures to
   a) add two matrices,
   b) subtract two matrices,
   c) multiply a matrix by a constant.

*3. Write functions to
   a) produce the largest element in a specified row of a matrix,
   b) produce the largest element in a specified column of a matrix,
   c) produce the largest element in a matrix.

*4. A "magic" square of order n is an n by n array of integers with the property that the numbers in each row, each column and both diagonals add up to the same "magic" number. If n is odd. a magic square containing the integers 1, 2, ..., n^2 can be generated by placing the value an+b in row i and column j of the square where

$$a = (n + j - i + (n-1) \text{ DIV } 2) \text{ MOD } n$$

and

$$b = 1 + (2j - i + n - 1) \text{ MOD } n$$

Write a procedure to generate a magic square of a given (odd) order.

5. Write a boolean function to determine whether a square array constitutes a "magic" square. Incorporate this procedure within a program to check that the squares produced by your program of exercise 4 are "magic".

*6. Incorporate your procedure of exercise 4 within a program to print a magic square and run the program with several different (odd) orders. In each magic square, observe the pattern followed by successive integers 1, 2, ... Write a procedure which produces a magic square by simply following this pattern and which makes no reference to the formulae of exercise 4.
   Note that this procedure works methodically through the numbers 1 to n^2 and its movement around the square is essentially diagonal, whereas the procedure of exercise 4 moves methodically (row-wise or column-wise) around the square but does not generate the integers 1 to n^2 in their natural sequence.

7. Write a boolean function to determine whether two supplied square arrays are equal (that is, they have the same value in corresponding positions). Incorporate this function in a program to check that the magic squares produced by your solutions to exercises 4 and 6 agree.

8. The game of Life {published in 'Scientific American', 223(4), 1970}
   simulates the life cycle of a society of living organisms. The
   society exists in an infinite two-dimensional array of cells, each
   cell having eight cells adjacent. Births and deaths occur
   simultaneously as each new generation is produced.
       A birth occurs in an empty cell with exactly three neighbours
   (occupied cells); the occupant of a cell with two or three
   neighbours survives to the next generation; the occupants of all
   other cells die from either isolation or overcrowding. So, if the
   initial society comprises four members forming a triangle in
   adjacent cells the next four generations display the following
   patterns.

   ```
                      *       *
     *    ***   * *   *     ***
    ***   ***         * *   * *
           *    ***   *     ***
                      *

     0     1    2     3      4
   ```

   In general, three eventual outcomes are possible.

      (i) The society becomes extinct.

      (ii) A steady state is reached: **
                                               **

      (iii) The society oscillates: *
                                          ***   *   ***   ...
                                                    *

   Write a program which accepts an initial configuration and displays
   successive patterns until either a steady state is reached or some
   predetermined number of generations has been produced.
       Adopt a finite space and assume that no organism can live beyond
   the boundary.

*9. Define an algorithm for optimal noughts and crosses play (tic tac
   toe). Represent the board by a two-dimensional array with rows and
   columns subscripted from −1 to 1. Write a program which implements
   your algorithm and play against your program.

10. Write a program to produce a forest scene composed of Christmas
   trees. Each tree is to comprise three triangles supported by a
   rectangular trunk. The vertex of each of the lower two triangles is
   to reach the mid-point of the triangle above it and each triangle
   is to be half as big again as the one above it.
       Your program should include a procedure to draw a tree and this
   should take, as parameters, the position of the top of the tree and
   the approximate overall height.

CHAPTER 16
This Must Be a Record

The first data types we met were the predefined <u>scalar</u> types (boolean, char, integer and real) and we went on to define scalar types of our own (symbolic and subrange). Then we met two <u>structured</u> types (files and arrays). A file is a collection of things all of the same type and stored in some order. If we want to find one component, we have to start at the front of the file and work through until we reach the thing we want. An array is also a collection of things all of the same type and stored in some order but, to pick out one component, we supply a subscript (or set of subscripts) and this gives us <u>dynamic</u> access in that the subscripts are evaluated at run-time. This chapter introduces a third structured type: the <u>record.</u>

A record is a collection of variables which need not all be of the same type and with no associated ordering. The variables are said to form <u>fields</u> of the record and we give every field of a record a name. Then, to pick out one component of a record, we use the name of the field. So, we use a record when we want to group values together but we do not need the dynamic access facility of an array. One example might be a date.

To represent a date, we would use three different types: one for days, one for months and one for the years (say from the year after the introduction of the Gregorian calendar to the year 2000).

```
TYPE
    days = 1 .. 31;
    months = (jan, feb, mar, apr, may, jun,
              jul, aug, sep, oct, nov, dec);
    years = 1583 .. 2000;
```

A date is a group of three values so a natural representation of a date is as a record with three fields.

```
dates =
    RECORD
        day : days;
        month : months;
        year : years
    END (* dates *);
```

A record definition starts with the word RECORD and finishes with the word END and, in between, we list the field identifiers. The order of the field identifiers is irrelevant but no two can be the same. The type of each field identifier must be specified and, as usual, the type is preceded by a colon. The field definitions are separated by semicolons and it is customary to follow the END by a comment.

If two fields are of the same type, a shorthand notation may be applied. As with ordinary declarations, the type need be quoted once and preceded by a list of identifiers. The two record types

```
        complex =
          RECORD
            realpart, imagpart : real
          END (* complex *);
```

and

```
        complex =
          RECORD
            realpart : real;
            imagpart : real
          END (* complex *);
```

are equivalent.

16.1 Record variables

Returning to the earlier example, we can use the type "dates" in a
declaration.

```
        VAR
          date : dates;
```

The variable "date" can be regarded as a single variable of type "dates"
and, for example, can have its value assigned to another "dates"
variable or written to a file of "dates"; or it can be regarded as three
variables and each component variable can be picked out individually. To
select one component from a record, we use its field name preceded by
the name of the record and the two must be separated by a dot. For
example, to set up the date May 17th 1994, we would use three
assignments: one to each component variable.

```
        date.month := may;
        date.day := 17;
        date.year := 1994
```


16.2 With-statement

In the above example, all the fields referred to in successive
statements belong to the same record variable. This is often the case
and so Pascal offers a shorthand notation. Rather than quote the name of
the record variable every time, we need use it only once, using a with-
statement.

```
        WITH date DO
        BEGIN
          month := may;   day := 17;   year := 1994
        END
```

These three assignments have exactly the same effect as before.

16.3 Record parameters

Records can be passed as parameters to procedures and functions. Figure 16.1 illustrates this. Given today's date, the procedure updates it to tomorrow's.

```
PROCEDURE Tomorrow (VAR date : dates);

    (* Updates today's date to tomorrow's *)

  FUNCTION atmonthend (date : dates) : boolean;
    FUNCTION leap (y : years) : boolean;
    BEGIN
      leap := (y MOD 400 = 0) OR
              (y MOD 4 = 0) AND (y MOD 100 <> 0)
    END (* leap *);
  BEGIN (* at month end *)
    WITH date DO
    CASE month OF
      sep, apr, jun, nov :
        atmonthend := day = 30;
      jan, mar, may, jul, aug, oct, dec :
        atmonthend := day = 31;
      feb :
        IF leap (year) THEN
          atmonthend := day = 29
        ELSE
          atmonthend := day = 28
    END (* CASE *)
  END (* at month end *);

BEGIN (* Tomorrow *)
  IF atmonthend (date) THEN
  WITH date DO
  BEGIN
    day := 1;
    IF month = dec THEN
    BEGIN
      month := jan;   year := year + 1
    END ELSE
      month := succ (month)
  END ELSE
    date.day := date.day + 1
END (* Tomorrow *);
```

                          Figure 16.1

Remember that, when a parameter is passed by value, a local copy is constructed and this can be costly in both time and space if the parameter is large so the comments made in section 14.3 concerning array parameters apply equally to records containing fields of array type. Note also that a record containing a field of any file type cannot be transferred as a value parameter (because files cannot be transferred as value parameters).

```
CONST
  maxidlength = 6;     maxnamelength = 50;
  maxaddline = 6;      maxstock = 1000;

TYPE
  stocklevels = 0 .. maxstock;
  orderlevels = 1 .. maxstock;
  idranges = 1 .. maxidlength;
  idents = PACKED ARRAY [idranges] OF char;
  nameranges = 1 .. maxnamelength;
  names = PACKED ARRAY [nameranges] OF char;
  addlines = 1 .. maxaddlines;
  addresses = ARRAY [addlines] OF names;
  sources =
    RECORD
         name : names;
      address : addresses
    END (* sources *);
  months = (jan, feb, mar, apr, may, jun,
            jul, aug, sep, oct, nov, dec);
  categories =
    (cat, dog, rabbit, mouse, bird, fowl, duck,
     spider, snake, alligator, food, medecine, miscellaneous);
  dates =
    RECORD
       day : 1 .. 31;
     month : months;
      year : 1900 .. 2000
    END (* dates *);
  orders =
    RECORD
         date : dates;
          qty : orderlevels;
         cost : real;
       source : sources;
     received : boolean
    END (* orders *);
  stocks =
    RECORD
          ident : idents;
           kind : categories;
           name : names;
       supplier : sources;
     qtyinstock : stocklevels;
      lastorder : orders;
     cost, price : real
    END (* stocks *);
  stockfiles = FILE OF stocks;
```

Figure 16.2

16.4 Files of records

One of the most important applications of record types is as the component type of a file because, when information is held in a file, it usually comprises a series of groups of facts. For example, two typical applications of computers are stock control and payroll calculation.

To monitor stock levels in a warehouse, a computer needs a file of facts about each item stored – the reference number of the item, the price of the item, the name and address of the supplier, the quantity in stock, the date of the last delivery and so on. To work out a payroll, it would need information about every employee – the department, salary, tax code and so on. To set up these files, we would define a record type to contain all the information we need about one item or one person and then we would construct a file of these records.

To illustrate this, we consider a simple stock control system for a pet shop. Figure 16.2 shows the declarations that might be used to define the master stock file. This not only illustrates a file of records, it also shows how record definitions can be nested. The record type "stocks" contains a field of type "orders" which is itself a record type and contains a field of type "dates" which is also a record type. The order of some of these declarations is important. A type cannot be referred to until it has been declared so the declaration of "dates" must precede the declaration of "orders" which, in turn, must precede "stocks".

To construct a stock file or to add some new items to a stock file we would write a program which reads from a text file, information about each new item, sets up a record for each new item and then updates the existing stock file to produce a new stock file including the new records.

Records in a stock file would be stored in some particular order, say in order of identification code. Assuming this to be the case, and assuming that the new items are presented in order of identification code, the program of figure 16.3 extends a master stock file. If an item is already present, the new information replaces the old and notification is given at the terminal.

So much for setting up a stock file – but this is not the only file we will need. At regular intervals we will have to run a program to update the master file in the light of all the transactions that have taken place during that period. So, we will need a program to generate a transaction file and one to read this and update the master file. Figure 16.4 shows the data types that might be used to define a transaction file.

A program to generate a transaction file would have a form similar to that of figure 16.3 but for transaction records rather than stock records. Records in the transaction file should refer to items in the same order as they are referred to in the master file. The program of figure 16.5 gives the form of a master file update program.

```pascal
PROGRAM StockExtend
    (stocksource, oldmaster, newmaster, output);

  CONST
    (* all the constants of figure 16.2 *)

  TYPE
    (* all the types of figure 16.2 *)

  VAR
    stocksource : text;
    oldmaster, newmaster : stockfiles;
    state : (scanning, found, passed, ateof);
    item : stocks;

  PROCEDURE GetNewItem (VAR stock : stocks);
    (* reads from "stocksource" and sets up a stock record *)
  BEGIN
    . . .
  END (* Get new item *);

BEGIN (* program body *)
  reset (stocksource);   reset (oldmaster);   rewrite (newmaster);
  REPEAT
    GetNewItem (item);
    state := scanning;
    REPEAT
      IF eof (oldmaster) THEN state := ateof ELSE
        IF oldmaster^.ident = item.ident THEN state := found ELSE
          IF oldmaster^.ident > item.ident THEN state := passed ELSE
          BEGIN
            write (newmaster, oldmaster^);   get (oldmaster)
          END
    UNTIL state <> scanning;

    IF state = found THEN
    BEGIN
      writeln (output, 'Item found');   get (oldmaster)
    END;

    write (newmaster, item)
  UNTIL eof (stocksource);

  WHILE NOT eof (oldmaster) DO
  BEGIN
    write (newmaster, oldmaster^);   get (oldmaster)
  END;
  writeln (output, 'Master file extended')
END.
```

Figure 16.3

```
CONST
  maxidlength = 6;    maxstock = 1000;

TYPE
  idranges = 1 .. maxidlength;
  transtypes = (sale, receipt, loss, gain);
  idents = PACKED ARRAY [idranges] OF char;
  orderlevels = 1 .. maxstock;
  transactions =
    RECORD
      ident : idents;
      qty : orderlevels;
      sort : transtypes
    END (* transactions *);
  transfiles = FILE OF transactions;
```

Figure 16.4

Notice that this program assumes that the transaction file data is correct. In a practical situation the program should check that items referred to by a transaction record do actually exist in the stock file.

16.5 Packed records

As with arrays (see section 14.2.1), information within a record can be packed. To achieve this, the word RECORD in the declaration must be preceded by the word PACKED. Use of packed records can reduce the amount of data space needed by a program but run-time speed may be adversely affected. In a context where records are handled in their entirety (eg assignment of a record to a variable) the use of a packed record may slightly improve run-time speed but, where individual fields are being selected from a record, run-time speed will be reduced.

16.6 Record variants

From the discussion of records so far it is apparent that all variables of the same record type have the same structure (that is, the same number of fields and the same field names). However it is possible to include variants within a record definition and then variables of the same record type can have different structures. Further, one record variable can have different structures at different times during the execution of a program.

A description of record variants is beyond the scope of this book.

```
    PROGRAM MasterUpdate
        (oldmaster, trans, newmaster, output);

      CONST
        (* all the constants of figures 16.2 and 16.4 *)

      TYPE
        (* all the types of figures 16.2 and 16.4 *)

      VAR
        oldmaster newmaster : stockfiles;
        trans : transfiles;
        stock : stocks;

      PROCEDURE Update (VAR st : stocks;  tran : transactions);
        (* Updates the stock record "st" in the
           light of the transaction record "tran" *)
      BEGIN
        . . .
      END (* Update *) ;

    BEGIN
      reset (oldmaster);   reset (trans);   rewrite (newmaster);
      REPEAT
        WHILE trans^.ident <> oldmaster^.ident DO
        BEGIN
          write (newmaster, oldmaster^);   get (oldmaster)
        END;
        read (oldmaster, stock);   Update (stock, trans^);
        write (newmaster, stock);   get (trans)
      UNTIL eof (trans);

      WHILE NOT eof (oldmaster) DO
      BEGIN
        write (newmaster, oldmaster^);  get (oldmaster)
      END;
      writeln (output, 'Stock update complete')
    END.
```

Figure 16.5

16.7 Exercises

*1. Modify your solution to exercise 10.5.11 to utilize a record type
to represent complex numbers.

2.   a) Define a record type to hold a person's name, date of birth,
sex and marital status (married, single, divorced, bereaved).
       b) Write a procedure to marry two people on a specified date.
The procedure should check that both are eligible for marriage: old
enough, of opposite sex and not already married. If the marriage is
permissable, the procedure must update the status of both partners
and change the woman's surname.

*3.   a) Define a record type with three fields to represent the time
of day in the usual twelve hour format (eg 10.47 am).
       b) Modify your solution to exercise 3.3.10 to utilize this type.

*4. Implement an enquiry system for a car saleroom. Define a record
type to represent a car by storing the make, model, registration
number, engine size, colour, price and insurance rating and then
write two programs to process a file of such records.
     One program is to read details of cars from a text file and
construct/amend a stock file, much along the lines of figure 16.3.
     The second is to allow a user to interrogate this file. The
program prompts the customer to specify his requirements and then
lists details of all appropriate cars in stock. If an aspect is of
no importance to the customer, nothing is typed apart from the end-
of-line character. Thus, to obtain a list of all vehicles costing
between $6000 and $7000 with engine capacities between 1000cc and
1350cc the responses, together with the prompts, could be as
follows.

```
              make :
             model :
   min engine size : 1000
   max engine size : 1350
max insurance rating :
            colour :
         min price : $6000
         max price : $7000
```

Appendix

RESERVED WORDS

Reserved words cannot be used as identifiers.

AND	DOWNTO	IF	OR	THEN
ARRAY	ELSE	IN	PACKED	TO
BEGIN	END	LABEL	PROCEDURE	TYPE
CASE	FILE	MOD	PROGRAM	UNTIL
CONST	FOR	NIL	RECORD	VAR
DIV	FUNCTION	NOT	REPEAT	WHILE
DO	GOTO	OF	SET	WITH

PREDEFINED IDENTIFIERS

These identifiers could be redefined within a Pascal program but this would usually be a foolish thing to do.

Constants

false   maxint   true

Types

boolean   char   integer   real   text

Files

input   output

Procedures

dispose	new	page	read	reset	unpack	writeln
get	pack	put	readln	rewrite	write	

Functions

abs	cos	exp	ord	sin	succ
arctan	eof	ln	pred	sqr	trunc
chr	eoln	odd	round	sqrt	

OPERATORS

For the purpose of defining operators, any operand of type s, where s is a subrange of type t, is treated as if it were of type t. Some operators can be applied to sets (which are available in greater generality than they have been covered in the book) and some to pointers (which have not been covered at all in the book).

Arithmetic operators

Operator	Operation	Type of operands	Type of result
+	addition	integer/real	integer/real
-	subtraction	integer/real	integer/real
*	multiplication	integer/real	integer/real
/	division	integer/real	real
DIV	integer division	integer	integer
MOD	modulo reduction	integer	integer

The operators + (identity) and - (negation) may also be used with only one operand. For any arithmetic operator, the result is of type real if an operand is of type real.

Boolean operators

Each boolean operator requires its operand(s) to be of type boolean and produces a result of type boolean.

Operator	Number of operands	Operation
NOT	1	logical inversion
AND	2	logical AND
OR	2	logical OR

Relational operators

Each relational operator requires two operands and produces a result of type boolean. With the exception of IN, both operands must have the same type (subject to the earlier comment regarding subranges).

Operator	Operation	Type of operands
=	equal to	real, ordinal, string, set
<>	not equal to	real, ordinal, string, set
<	less than	real, ordinal, string
>	greater than	real, ordinal, string
<=	less than or equal to	real, ordinal, string, set
>=	greater than or equal to	real, ordinal, string, set
IN	set membership	left : some ordinal type t right: SET OF t

Priorities of operators

1 {highest}	:	NOT
2	:	*	/	DIV	MOD	AND
3	:	+	-	OR
4 {lowest}	:	=	<>	<	>	<=	>=	IN

Subject to these priorities and to the effect of brackets, operators are applied from left to right.

THE ASCII CHARACTER SET

In the table below, the ordinal number of a character is the sum of its row number and column number. The space character has ordinal number 32 and all the other caps correspond to "control characters" which have no printable representation.

	0	1	2	3	4	5	6	7	8	9	10	11	12	13	14	15
0																
16																
32		!	"	#	$	%	&	'	(	)	*	+	,	-	.	/
48	0	1	2	3	4	5	6	7	8	9	:	;	<	=	>	?
64	@	A	B	C	D	E	F	G	H	I	J	K	L	M	N	O
80	P	Q	R	S	T	U	V	W	X	Y	Z	[	\	]	^	_
96	£	a	b	c	d	e	f	g	h	i	j	k	l	m	n	o
112	p	q	r	s	t	u	v	w	x	y	z	{	|	}	~	

Index